THE BEST IS YET TO COME

A Memoir about Football and Finding a Way through the Dark

ALAN O'MARA

First published in Ireland in 2016 by
HACHETTE BOOKS IRELAND

1

Cataloguing in Publication Data is available from the British Library

ISBN 9781473648296

Typeset in Century Gothic by redrattledesign.com

Printed and bound in Great Britain by Clays Ltd, St Ives plc

Hachette Books Ireland policy is to use papers that are natural, renewable
and recyclable products and made from wood grown in sustainable forests.
The logging and manufacturing processes are expected to conform to the
environmental regulations of the country of origin.

Hachette Books Ireland
8 Castlecourt Centre
Castleknock
Dublin 15, Ireland

A division of Hachette UK Ltd
Carmelite House, 50 Victoria Embankment,
London EC4Y 0DZ

www.hachettebooksireland.ie

To my parents, Carol and Michael,
and my brothers, Billy and David

Thank you for your unconditional love and support
through good times and bad

Contents

Prologue
The Night

As the hours ticked by, I grew more and more self-conscious. I was expending most of my energy forcing the tears in my eyes back down the pipes they had risen up, a special talent I had developed. The familiar voices that surrounded me intertwined naturally, and as the many strands of conversations and stories flowed effortlessly from my friends, I fought the sporadic urge to cry. Unfortunately, they weren't the tears of laughter that everyone else seemed to be sharing.

'Remember that time you tipped your car into a snowman for the laugh?' one said. Someone pulled out a phone to relive the moment once more, and everyone burst out laughing at the video. I faked a chuckle. I was there in body among my closest friends, but not in mind or spirit. I was somewhere else, a dark and confusing place.

I focused on trying to get to grips with the feelings rushing around inside my body and mind, but I had become a master of putting on a mask and keeping my emotions hidden. Conversations sailed over my head.

I managed to give the impression of being actively involved in the chatter by cracking a half-smile every now and again, or swallowing a mouthful of beer. Sometimes I would muster a half-hearted laugh, or simply nod my head like one of those toy dogs in the rear window of a car – bopping along for the amusement of others. The heat in the pub had water running from my hairline down the sides of my face and an unattractive wet patch had formed under each armpit.

Everyone else stood there interacting effortlessly, engaging and mingling with one another, which only added to my self-consciousness. Why can't I feel like them? Why couldn't I enjoy my Christmas? Everyone else made it look so easy.

Elation and festive spirit visibly filled body after body around the L-shaped bar, like an electric surge. Even though the heat was intense, I knew I was sweating more than normal for somebody as athletic as myself. I began to worry that the sweat would transform into an odour that would attract more attention. I just didn't feel the same as everyone else. Throughout the evening I drank, one pint after the other, trying to keep up my happy demeanour as I stood with the group, waiting for the alcohol to kick in and help me escape the feelings of numbness and sadness.

I had felt like this before.

I knew what was going on, but that didn't make it any easier. I didn't want to feel this way again. My stomach rumbled. I had a mild headache and my back hurt from being crouched on a barstool with no back support all evening. I headed for the exit. The cold air that greeted me when I pushed open the glass-panelled door was soothing, and its iciness matched how I was feeling inside.

The bubbly, warm, cheerful mood that filled the pub failed to extend even a foot beyond the entrance. I closed the door behind me and took a few short steps away in search of solace. I wanted to close my eyes, to take a few deep breaths and ask the headache that was now dominating my brain to kindly leave. 'It's Christmas. You have to enjoy Christmas,' I muttered to myself.

As I stood motionless in a world of my own, I panicked and started to wonder if anybody was watching me as I went through this episode. I checked, but I was alone – alone except for one mysterious creature I knew all too well. It was looming over me, and slowly but surely draining my soul from the vessel that carried it. While drinking had helped to keep me distracted throughout the evening, the alcohol hadn't kept the internal conversations in my head at bay. Despite being surrounded by my best friends and my girlfriend all evening, I felt isolated and alone, irrelevant once again.

I was tired of having to put up with all the dark emotions I was feeling and thoughts I was juggling when everybody else seemed to be having such effortless fun. I stormed off into the night in search of my bed.

'Ah, young O'Mara, how are things? Are you back with Cavan this year?' I was asked as I plodded down the path of the town's Main Street.

'Not so bad, lad, getting on grand,' I said, before ignorantly ploughing on and pretending I hadn't heard the second question. I was in no mood to talk football.

With the number of taxis in Bailieborough struggling to cope with the increased population in the town for the festive season, I took a notion to walk home – all three miles of a dark, meandering country road. I needed to get away from where I had been. Anywhere was better than there because I could no longer pretend to be happy in front of everyone.

I wandered out of the town and past the fields, taking no heed of time, drifting farther and farther from the party and my friends. I went deeper into the darkness and cold, happy in the knowledge that every step I took seemed like one more away from the anxiety and pain I had been enduring all evening.

I couldn't take one more second of it. I wanted it to be gone.

I wanted my brain to slow down. I wanted to feel happy for a few minutes. Even just for one minute. All I wanted was a short reprieve from my inner torture. *Please just go away and let me enjoy Christmas like everybody else. Can you not let me be happy?*

I yearned for another state of mind as I drifted through the night. Goose pimples had taken over my whole body, but the cold proved to be only a temporary distraction from the conversations running on a loop in my mind. I was angry at having to endure so much confusion within me and couldn't understand why I felt the way I did. I wished there were an 'off' switch.

The road I was walking along seemed abandoned; there was little or no sign of life anywhere. It was bitterly cold. Limb-numbing, nose-reddening, puddle-freezing cold. The only sign of life was the twinkle of festive lights in the distance. However, all they did was remind me of the glow of the pub and all the acting I'd had to do to survive in its nauseating warmth. It was better to go it alone. I would keep to the side of the road until I got home to bed and could put an end to this miserable night.

The two distinct voices in my head were in full flight again, arguing and debating what had become of my life, but the negative voice was so much more prominent. *Who am I? What is the point of all this? Do I even know what makes me happy? Will I ever feel happy again? Will this always be looming over me? Should I go back to counselling? Does it actually help, or am I just prolonging the inevitable – suicide?*

This was the catalyst for tears. They lined up and held on – right on the edge of crossing from my world into the real world. They began to blur my vision and fill to my heavy eyelids. The urge to let them out was overwhelming but the dam trapping the water wouldn't buckle under the pressure.

In the distance, lights seemed to be getting closer. The edges of the beams were making their way through a hedge, but I couldn't identify the source. I kept walking and the light just kept getting closer. I was drawn to it as if it were a magnet. *Or maybe I was the magnet.* I grew frustrated at yet another pointless conversation buzzing around inside my head. Nobody could hear these conversations, or the effects of the constant back-and-forth, the endless doubts they threw up, but I was living with them all the time. I'd listen to them, passively, watching it all play out in my own mind as clear as any film I had ever seen on a giant cinema screen.

All of a sudden, the road ahead was ablaze with light as a car came around the corner. I felt numb inside and out, and being jolted out of my internal dialogue reminded me about just how cold I was. The light seemed so warm and inviting that I was really drawn to it. I thought of holding my hand up to get a lift, to lift me out of the place I found myself in, but then I remembered the tears in my eyes and how pathetic I must have looked.

That sinister voice in my head suggested something else to get me out of this situation. I clearly imagined throwing myself in front of the oncoming car and letting it knock me out of this world. I wasn't dreaming or, more accurately, having a nightmare. I was wide awake, and it seemed like such a normal thing to do. It felt like it would be such a logical choice in that moment.

Jump. Bang. Gone.

What a good way to make sure I never had to listen to the crap in my head again. I took half a step towards the middle of the road, but instead of yielding to the magnetic pull of the car, I dropped my shoulder like Larry Reilly, the famous Cavan forward renowned for jinking past defenders, and went the other way. I flung myself behind a nearby wall and slumped miserably to the ground. The alcohol in my system was quickly overpowered by the adrenaline pumping through my body. I snapped out of my drunken, confused haze in an instant.

I remained hidden for several minutes down on my hunkers, so angry that I wanted to punch myself in the head. Instead I slammed my fist into my upper leg and then hit out at the concrete wall that concealed me. I couldn't believe how close I had come to ending my life. I told myself that I was never going to drink alcohol again – it was to blame for my overriding compulsion to sling myself in front of an oncoming car.

It took all my willpower not to burst into tears as I conjured up a painful memory from my past. This wasn't the first suicidal moment I had survived.

1

The Awakening

My body shook uncontrollably as a searing and repetitive pain shot through my midriff. Moving made it worse, and I squeezed the unfamiliar bed frame in search of some sort of comfort. The nurse beside my bed spotted my distress and finally came to my aid. After fiddling with some equipment she told me she had pumped more morphine into my system, but the pain was unrelenting. She tried to distract me by making conversation, but talking only made the pain worse.

I lay there and stared at the ceiling; manners were certainly not at the top of my list of priorities. Unfortunately there was absolutely nothing up there to entertain me as the pain overpowered every thought in my head. Everything I tried to say came out sounding like I had a bad stammer. I started to breathe heavily, and the more I moved my diaphragm, the worse the pain became. There was an oxygen mask covering my mouth and I sucked in air like I was a rookie diver about to submerge myself underwater. I was panicking.

The nurse, in her wisdom, warned me to slow down my breathing; if I didn't, I would hyperventilate. Did she really think telling me that was going to calm me down? Did she think I was doing it on purpose? I didn't want to talk anyway – the pain was eating me up. It was all I could think about. My body was on fire on the inside, like it was about to implode.

Finally she injected extra morphine in an effort to help my body relax. I gestured for more.

'I'm sorry, but I have already given you the maximum dosage allowed. You should start to feel better in the next few minutes. Just sit tight,' she said.

Slowly but surely I felt the drug seep through my veins and infiltrate my body. The pain eased. A soothing numbness spread over me, and it was such a welcome relief.

I drifted in and out of consciousness as the narcotic began to take its toll. My eyes gave up the fight and closed. I was woken by someone shaking my arm: a different nurse. I was no longer as high as a kite and had regained control of my senses.

I remembered where I was and what had happened. It was November 2010 and I was lying in a bed in the day ward of the Hermitage Medical Clinic, Dublin, having just undergone surgery that was going to make or break my football career. I was 20 years old. I knew I wasn't going to be able to go on the way I had been over the course of the previous two years. A string of injuries and constant pain had severely restricted my development as a goalkeeper. A mysterious pain had regularly shifted between my lower back, groin and quad, and no one had been able to figure out what was causing it.

This had gone on for so long without proper diagnosis that I sometimes wondered if I was imagining it all. I had first been sent to a renowned groin surgeon in mid-2010, but after a quick examination, during which I explained to the doctor that the pain was not always in the same place, I was told that surgery was not an option. I was given a generic running programme to complete – which I never did. I left feeling bitterly disappointed at how brief our conversation had been, and remained adamant that something really was wrong. Not everyone believed me though, and I knew people thought I was being a drama queen.

'You could always try an injection of water into it to see if that makes a difference,' said one official from my club, Bailieborough Shamrocks, as I stood on the edge of the athletics track and watched the rest of the guys train in the freezing cold. I walked away in disgust. He clearly thought it was all in my head and that I needed to man up, but I knew how my body felt and that there was something seriously wrong. I needed answers.

It didn't help that X-rays on my back and MRI scans of my groin and thigh muscles revealed no clear problem other than inflammation around the pubic bone caused by repetitive stress and overuse – which is quite common in athletes. The typical treatment is a steroid injection into the pubic bone joint and a couple of weeks' rest and recovery.

While that explained some of my discomfort and alleviated part of the pain, the main issue that had been hampering me for two years and resulted in being heavily strapped for training and playing games remained unresolved. My right leg was so often covered with sticky bandages that I'd shaved the top part to make removing them less taxing. Not a day went by when my back didn't hurt either. I had a constant ache while driving, and one night, as I was warming up before training with the Cavan senior team as an 18-year-old, I had felt a pain shooting up either side of my spine every time I took a step. That had scared me.

Now, I couldn't help but wonder if I would ever find the answers I needed. Was I going to have to retire in my early twenties? Was I going to be a washed-up has-been at such a young age? It was a notion I couldn't even begin to contemplate, so I began to research surgery options online. After my surgery consultation, I considered flying to Germany to visit one of Europe's leading clinics.

I was only in this predicament because I had pushed myself so hard – both by continually playing through the pain barrier and holding back in training so that I could carry on playing in major games, which the coaches and physio supported me in doing. I loved playing and nothing else in my life came close to matching it, and I'd do anything to protect my game time for club or county. At times I was chewing painkillers like they were sweets, despite still being a teenager. I knew this wasn't normal, but I never once stopped to consider the negative effect they were having on my body. In my mind, I was just doing what had to be done. Taking painkillers out of the medicine cabinet in our family home seemed the best way to do that, even though they regularly upset my stomach. All I cared about was getting the sense of satisfaction that only sport could give me.

Now I wish that someone had pulled me aside when I was a teenager and helped me to improve the strength, durability and flexibility of my muscles, but, then again, I probably wouldn't have listened to them anyway.

In my early teenage years I'd thought I was bulletproof, and I wouldn't let anyone tell me otherwise. Instead of resting when I'd torn my right hamstring, my kicking leg, while playing under-16s with my club, I'd trained up my left leg to take kick-outs instead of accepting the limitations of the injury. We were playing against Redhills and I knew several of their players from playing with the underage county teams. They had looked at me like I had seven heads when they saw me running up and striking the ball with my left leg. 'You are some boy, O'Mara. Would you not have a day off?' one had said.

'I could, but then it would be too easy for you to score goals, sure,' I'd replied with a wink.

I'd done what I'd had to do to play, constantly focusing only on the next game and never thinking about the bigger picture.

I needed to play Gaelic football. Playing gave me a real sense of drive, purpose and belonging. I loved doing it, and it helped that I excelled at it too. I would train and play as often possible, sometimes squeezing in two matches on the one day. In 2007, when I was still just 16, I was playing in goal for six different teams – county minor, my school's under-16 and senior teams, and my club's minor, under-21 and senior teams – and I couldn't get enough of it.

I kept ploughing through the pain in my back, quad and groin until one night in 2010 when my body finally broke down in Mullingar. It was during the first half of a challenge match for Cavan under-21s against Clare's Kilmurry Ibrickane, who were preparing for an All-Ireland club final appearance. I had been struggling for most of the season and I was ordered to take time off with a view to getting match fit for our upcoming championship campaign. It was my last chance to hold on to my number one jersey at under-21 inter-county level for the second season in a row, straight after starting for the Cavan minors for two consecutive years. I knew nothing other than being number one for whatever Cavan team I was playing for.

As this was my comeback game against the Clare champions, my aim was to talk to my defence at least once every minute to make my presence felt – with both teammates and management. Most of the lads I played with over the years enjoyed that communication, the constant sense that I was switched on, in the zone and looking out for danger. When we lined up together, I focused fully on helping my team not concede scores.

After a scrappy start, the Munster champions had yet to really trouble our goals. My kick-outs were going fine. Seven steps back, two to the left; that was the routine I had engrained in my conscience since I was a child. I had spent countless hours mastering that run-up and striking technique. From having a bag of balls in my own back garden and kicking them through the white pebble-dashed pillars at our house, to the training pitch in Bailieborough and Kingspan Breffni Park, I gave my kick-out technique the same level of attention that a professional golfer gives his swing.

When the game started, I always forgot about the pain. There was just something special about standing in between the posts and taking my place on the team. I felt like it was what I was born to do and I was exactly where I needed to be. I loved the freedom of it all, being able to express myself in such a satisfying way, and I liked the headspace it took me to. I loved the pressure of being a goalkeeper, of being the last line of defence. The adrenaline would take over and delay any physical discomfort until after the match. More often than not, it was worse the following morning and I would grip the sheets to help myself get upright and out of bed.

Midway through the first half of the Kilmurry Ibrickane game, however, I knew some part of my body had given up on me. I started to feel slight numbness, as if I was no longer in full control of my limbs when I swung my leg at the ball. I kept forcing it, desperate to be able to take my place in the upcoming Ulster championship. But if I wanted the ball to go up the middle, it went right. If I aimed right, it would go over the sideline. If I shaped to go left, like I had practised so often, it would go up the middle. I just wasn't connecting with the ball the way I wanted to. I had lost my aim, and it was maddening. Out of pure stubbornness, I kept going, not understanding how a technique I had mastered so well could malfunction so badly.

When the half-time whistle sounded, I knew it wasn't happening for me, but I didn't ask to come off. I wasn't waving the flag on my championship ambitions that easily. There was no fooling the manager, Terry Hyland, however, who was only too aware that I wasn't performing. I was subbed – and I was devastated. I sat demoralised on the bench, a hunchbacked pile of misery.

'You all right there, AOM?' asked both Darragh Tighe and Oisin Minagh, two of the other substitutes, clearly noticing my distress. 'Get some gear on or you'll freeze, lad,' I heard, as a pair of O'Neills waterproof bottoms landed on my lap along with a jumper. I never bothered to look up to see who had thrown them. I gave a slight nod in thanks and remained speechless. I sat there sulking and feeling sorry for myself. My body had finally given up, but my mind wasn't able to accept it.

~

After months of frustration and searching for a cure since that cold night in Mullingar, I found the answer to my problem in Ailbe McCormack, a former physio with the Ireland rugby team. Ronan Carolan, a Cavan legend and physio with the Cavan under-21 team, had recommended him in a bid to get to the bottom of my mysterious pains.

But as I failed to make progress after weeks of sticking rigidly to his programme, Ailbe reached the conclusion that what I really needed was hernia repair surgery, and referred me to a surgeon, Michael Allen, who was confident he could provide the much-needed solution, after a physical exam that involved some intense poking of fingers into sensitive parts of my midriff. The sports hernia I had developed was a soft-tissue injury to my lower abdomen, but unlike regular hernias, these rarely show a visible bulge, which makes them more difficult to detect. In addition, my MRI scan and X-rays continued to look normal, with none of the symptoms showing up on either.

I longed to get back to pushing my body to its limits instead of dreading the inevitable pain. I had no other option but to trust the opinions of both the surgeon and physio. It was 'win or bust' for me, as time was running out to get fit for the new season. Having missed out on so much football in 2010, I was all in. I needed to get back training, get back to my team and my friends. As I looked forward to playing my last under-21 season with Cavan after missing out on the 2010 Ulster final defeat to Donegal, I felt the desire to become the best goalkeeper in the country burning within me once again. It was both my dream and my plan.

Thankfully, 2011 brought a whole new set of competitions, and I had the opportunity to put my frustrations and disappointments behind me. I was determined to kick on and become the goalkeeper I was meant to be – the goalkeeper that goalkeeping coaches Aaron Donohoe and Paul O'Dowd, two former Cavan keepers with whom I had worked a lot in my teenage years, passionately believed I could become. I had a colossal amount of gym work to get through, hundreds of hours of monotonous, mind-numbing and repetitive exercises post-surgery, but lying in the hospital bed, I was only thinking about the months ahead and the opportunities they would bring.

I simply had to play with the Cavan under-21s in 2011; it was my last chance to play in my own age group. I had to make it back. I had to be part of the team, had to play with that group of lads. Since I had met most of them when I was 14, I felt like I belonged with them. I remember the day the letter arrived informing me that I had successfully secured a place on the Cavan under-14 development squad. I beamed with pride after reading it several times.

Still just 13, I got on a bus at seven one morning in Virginia knowing only Sean Cooney, a school friend, and was introduced immediately to Colm Smith from Kingscourt Stars, a neighbouring club to my Bailieborough Shamrocks. The two lads already knew each other and I quickly struck up a good relationship with Colm. To this day, the three of us are still great friends, even though Colm is living in London, where he works as a strength and conditioning coach with Harlequins rugby club. Apart from those two, I knew nobody. But I didn't need to know anyone else; as far as I was concerned, all I had to do was stand in goals and stop the ball going past me. The rest would figure itself out in time.

I slotted in seamlessly to a group that was heavily dominated by players who attended St Pat's College in Cavan. Something just clicked that day for me. I was so grateful to be part of that team, and we had to win an Ulster championship to put an end to the embarrassing drought that was ruining a county steeped in so much history.

We were determined that the disappointment we'd felt at minor level in 2008 could not be repeated. That feeling of emptiness after losing an Ulster semi-final, when we took a one-point lead into the dying minutes against Tyrone only to let it slip away, haunted us all. It was worse again when we had to watch them become All-Ireland minor champions following a replay against a Mayo side inspired by Aidan O'Shea.

I couldn't take that hurt again. Somebody had to help revive Cavan football from its slumber and I knew our bunch could do it. I couldn't wait for the adventure to begin.

All of this raced through my head as I lay in the hospital nursing the fresh wound in my lower abdomen. The surgery had been the next step on my path to achieving those dreams. After getting out of the hospital bed with the help of a nurse, in a gown that flashed my bum, I got dressed and prepared to return to Cavan.

I had to be careful not to disturb any of the bandaging that was around my waist, but I made that journey home with my father Michael and younger brother Billy. I was sore and tender and it hurt to move, but there in Bailieborough I rested, recovered fully and dreamt a little more of the possible glory days ahead in the Cavan jersey in 2011.

2
The Rise

During the winter of 2010, nothing invaded my brain more than the upcoming Ulster under-21 campaign. Santa Claus couldn't deliver this year – all I wanted was the piece of silverware that could only be earned the hard way.

That year I was living in Dublin with school friends as I studied Journalism in DIT. There were eight of us living in a house on Dublin's North Circular Road, of whom Barry Tully and Shane Gray were also on the panel. To say that football was a central pillar of our house would be an understatement and one day when I should have been in college, I found myself lying in my bedroom chatting to a friend and writing on my bed sheet with a pen what I thought would be the starting team.

'The full-back line is nailed down. Who do you think will be in the half-back line? There is definitely a spot up for grabs there,' I fished.

He wasn't sure how the team was going to take shape either, so I pressed on, trying to give it the shape I was hoping for.

'Yeah, the full-back line is sorted, lad – Oisin Minagh, Damien Barkey and Darragh Tighe. Kevin Meehan will be in the half-back line, but the other two slots are fairly open. Not sure who will be beside Gearoid McKiernan in the middle either,' I added. The reality was that I could think about it as much as I liked, but without a serious amount of work with the physio to prepare properly for a return to action, I was not going to be a part of it.

The couple of hours I'd spent in the operating theatre a month earlier had involved a mesh being placed into my abdomen to address the weakening of the muscles and tendons in my lower abdominal wall. I was travelling between Dublin and Cavan a lot but recovery was longer and more painful than I had anticipated, and it meant that without proper rehab my groin was unlikely to hold up for a full championship campaign where it needed to be able to survive the pressure of me kicking thousands of O'Neills footballs.

With that in mind I met Enda King, a physio in the renowned Sports Surgery Clinic in Santry, in the middle of December. He had come highly recommended by Ailbe McCormack to be the physio to monitor my recovery programme following the surgery, as Enda had recently gone through a similar operation himself. Within a short space of time I could feel I was definitely on the mend; I was back driving and walking comfortably enough. I was so committed to minding my body over those initial 14 days post surgery that I rarely stepped outside when the winter of 2010 brought heavy snowfall and no shortage of ice to Cavan. There was no way I was going to slip and suffer a setback. I clung to the safety of my house in Bailieborough and thanked my family for minding me. I was so focused on doing what had to be done to get back out on the field that I wrapped myself in cotton wool and took every ounce of rest I could get.

When I first met Enda King, he had gone through my whole body and tested the strength and flexibility of my quads, groin, abdomen, back and hips. It was obvious that these parts – which accounted for rather a lot of my body – had been under pressure for too long because of my commitment to the game. There was definite wear and tear, but he told me it was nothing that couldn't be fixed by hard work in the gym. Enda was a fine footballer who had won a number of county titles with Cavan Gaels at midfield but had suffered injury problems of his own. If anyone was going to understand the pains, niggles and problems I was going to suffer along the way, it was him.

I was starting at the foot of the mountain, and was delighted to have him as my guide on those first few steps. He went through simple exercises with me just to get my lower body ticking over again. Most of them were focused on basic core activation muscles in the abdomen, which are used during most movements of the body on a football field. These are the muscles that any athlete who has suffered injury will know about. The exercises focused on maintaining control of my core muscles while breathing in and out, then bringing in gradual movements of the legs. They are mind-numbingly boring, but chatting away to him I was optimistic. He knew from the off that I expected to be back playing in six weeks to give me a good chance at regaining form and being match-ready ahead of our opening under-21 Ulster championship quarter-final against Fermanagh in Brewster Park on 16 March.

Enda gave me a precise programme, with clear tallies for exercises, and he set goals that were going to improve the control in my core, the activation of my glutes and the mobility of my hips. Over the years I had developed a pelvic tilt, due to poor posture and core control, that was putting unnecessary pressure on other parts of my body when I moved at speed. We had to be very focused with our targets to correct those inadequacies, as our time window was shorter than that recommended by the surgeon.

Enda made it clear that if my results hadn't improved by my next visit, I would not be fit for the match in March. I loved that directness. He was exactly who I needed in order to get me going. It helped that he had Cavan football at heart too. Leaving the clinic one day before Christmas, he handed me a written list of everything we'd discussed, which we went through carefully to make sure I understood exactly what I had to do. 'This is your life for the next seven days,' he said.

I looked at him and laughed, but he didn't smile. He meant business.

So did I.

~

It was invigorating to get back into a team environment in January 2011 and to be in and around the group again after all the time I had spent alone recovering from surgery and improving my strength. I felt blessed to be in a team with such strong characters who were all working towards the same goal. The chemistry always seemed right within our group. We all knew that we had ability and were talented individuals, but our experiences over the years had taught us that we were even stronger together. We made each other better players.

My previous teams may have had natural ability – some would argue more – but the likes of Gearoid McKiernan, Niall Murray, Conor McClarey, Niall McDermott, Oisin Minagh, Colm Smith, Niall Smith, Barry Reilly, Kevin Meehan, Damien Barkey and Darragh Tighe were the men I wanted with me when we crossed the white line.

As my recovery from the surgery continued, I began togging out with the team, but when they took to the 3G pitch that was neatly tucked away at the back of Kingspan Breffni Park, I trotted to the gym upstairs to do my bit and keep working at Enda's prescriptive routine. They were only baby steps, but each one brought me closer to my Cavan jersey.

It was frustrating not to be out there with the rest of the team, but it was better than sitting at home doing the exercises by myself – that seriously tested my sanity and patience at times.

I had been doing them every day, constantly hearing Enda's words in my head and trusting that he was the man to get me right after years of disappointment and false dawns. But there were ups and downs, and one day I grew so frustrated, I punched a dent in the wall at home. Progress was slow, and all I wanted was to feel the buzz of making a save once more. As I sucked in my stomach and tried to activate my core, I could feel how weak I was. I knew that if I wasn't able to do it while I was lying down and fully focused on activating parts of my body, I had no chance of replicating the correct movement when training or executing 60-yard kicks. It wasn't working the way it had when Enda showed me, and it was more challenging to do the exercises correctly without his direct supervision and guidance. I was annoyed that I had to go through much more than others to take my place in our starting fifteen.

The exercises were all about quality, not quantity, and Enda told me that I was better off doing six correctly than 20 lethargically. I even made a stab at them on Christmas Day but gave up halfway through and ate a chocolate Kimberley – I'd earned it! Most days in the gym I had the company of Kevin Meehan, who was having injury troubles of his own. He was fantastic company. He's a human encyclopaedia – thoughtful and intelligent – and a real gentleman. Part of the reason I played football was to meet characters like him. He was also a good man to demand a short kick-out – and long before it became the fashionable thing to do.

On 3 January I was in Kingspan Breffni Park, not to play with my teammates but to stand on the sidelines and manage the Dublin Institute of Technology fresher football team against the under-21 side that I was so desperate to be a part of. Being in charge of the DIT team gave me something else to focus on in the months when I couldn't play. It was a fantastic experience over the three years I did it, and I got to coach the likes of Mayo's Aidan O'Shea, Monaghan's Colin Walshe, Meath's Bryan Menton and Westmeath's Kieran Martin, all magnificent footballers. We won an All-Ireland fresher championship in my first year working with Billy O'Loughlin from Laois and Paul Clancy, who had won two All-Irelands with Galway in 1998 and 2001.

It was certainly a strange experience, picking a line-up that would take on my own team, the other side of the pitch filled with the friends I wanted to play with. It was almost surreal standing on the sidelines with my DIT jacket on, pitting my wits against Terry Hyland and his management team of Anthony Forde, Joe McCarthy and Ronan Carolan – but I really enjoyed it. It was a novelty, but in a strange way I felt it put me right back on the radar of the management team and reminded them how important I could be to the side in terms of leadership and influence. Obviously they knew I was working hard to recover from the surgery, but as an injured player there is always a deep-down fear that they will forget about you – out of sight, out of mind. The Cavan line-up was fairly experimental but the game finished in a draw, which meant I didn't have to take any slagging from Terry. The whole experience made me want to get back playing even more. I loved coaching teams, managing and working with different players and personalities, but it was a different satisfaction to that of playing. Being a leader for other players, earning their trust and respect and helping them to be the best they could be was hugely rewarding, but I would be a liar if I said it came anywhere close to the feeling of being the Cavan goalkeeper.

After the game, when the DIT bus headed back to Dublin, I went to the gym upstairs and did more core work. I lifted my hampered leg up and down for 30 minutes and wondered how many more hours it would be before I was back out on the field. I knew I was getting there. Momentum kept gathering in my recovery, and it meant a lot to me that the management had faith to put me straight back into the team when I was declared fit. It added to my own conviction that I could make that journey from the operating theatre back into competitive action within four months but it wasn't all plain sailing.

One night while training with Enda King in Ringsend in Dublin, I had been left wondering if I still had what it took to play at the top level as he mercilessly hammered goal after goal past me. I told him I needed to go to the toilet and I went through the trees behind the goals and puked. I strolled back out into the goals and we went at it again. He was relentless, and I owe him a lot for what that relentlessness did for me.

When Enda gave me the thumbs-up to play a game in February 2011, my first match in almost a year, I wanted to jump up from the treatment table and hug him. For too long I had been lost in a world of uncertainty concerning my injuries, but now I was about to leave those struggles behind me. I was absolutely thrilled to be standing in the goals again, barking encouragement and instructions at my comrades. I didn't want to be anywhere else. I was where I belonged.

Our pre-championship programme ramped up in Mullagh when we played Dublin under-21s, the reigning All-Ireland champions, and it was a massive test for us to go up against one of the so-called 'big boys', who were managed by Jim Gavin. We dominated the first half and led 0-5 to 0-3 at the break. The heavy conditions underfoot hampered the brand of football either side could produce, but we showed our hunger and how hard we could work for each other. I was feeling much sharper compared to just two weeks previously when I had walked into the dressing room with my bag on my back, fully ready to play. Ronan Carolan, who was part of the Ulster-winning 1997 team, was double-jobbing as our team physio and selector and I think he was surprised to see me with my gear. He questioned whether I was ready to return just yet.

'I'm good to go, chief. Enda gave me the thumbs-up during the week. Time to get back on the horse,' I said firmly.

I pretended to be more confident than I actually was, but of course I had doubts after such a long time out. I didn't want anybody else to pick up on that, so I just tried to keep believing, like Terry had so often urged me to do.

Early in that game in Páirc Tailteann I had made two brilliant saves and the feeling was incredible. The exhilaration pumping through my body was out of this world. A part of me wanted to think I had made those saves, and so soon after my return, because I was so naturally talented and a great goalkeeper – but that really wasn't the case. I pulled off those saves because I had worked incredibly hard, like a man possessed, to enable me to chase my dream. In previous seasons I had definitely taken my ability for granted at different stages but that outstanding performance in Navan felt so much sweeter because I knew how hard I had worked to make it happen.

Despite the upturn in my form during the match against Meath in February, the second half against Dublin was very disappointing. We only scored one point and they completely ran the show. We had stopped fighting, and that is just not good enough in a county like Cavan for which few people outside our own group showed any respect – we had to go out and earn that respect each and every time. When we failed to work hard as a unit I honestly felt we were all wasting our time turning up for training and games on those cold, dark nights. That was the bare minimum for Cavan football. It had to be if we wanted to change things.

Towards the end of February we corrected that second-half collapse in a match against Armagh, but it was not without its complications. I had left Dublin at 5 p.m. in my car as the business end of our season loomed. I didn't go to college that day as I got myself some quality sleep and a belly full of chicken and pasta. Gearoid McKiernan, Oisin Minagh, Shane Gray and Barry Tully were all with me but as we got to Newry we could smell burning from the car. I turned off the heater and hoped it would go away but because the windows steamed up with the five of us on board, I had to put it back on, and we continued to get the burning smell. I checked the engine and realised there was no cap on the oil tank – obviously I hadn't put it back on properly when I topped up the levels earlier that week.

My car had already been struggling to handle the

miles I was racking up for my love of the county. On two people's recommendations I took off a sock and used it as a makeshift cover, and we ploughed on to the Athletic Grounds. I wasn't worried about the car; my focus was on arriving for the battle ahead.

We got there 45 minutes after everyone else but had enough time for a warm-up and to lace up the boots. I started that match, as did Gearoid and Oisin. For the full 60 minutes we put together an excellent cocktail of work rate, discipline, panache and spirit. We comfortably dispatched Armagh and looked razor sharp as a group heading in to our championship campaign. I knew that if we played like that for the rest of the season it was going to take an incredible team to beat us. My self-confidence and belief were growing all the time and I could feel it in the others too. We were starting to have a subtle swagger when we pulled on the blue uniform – and that was unheard of in Cavan.

After the match, content with our evening's work, I steered the car for Dublin after checking the sock and making sure it was still in place. We began the journey, but the car was not driving smoothly. I was so focused on discussing the game and the bigger picture that I failed to pay any real attention to the problems the engine was experiencing. As we cruised by Dundalk at 120 km/h, the car cut out after a loud bang and the power steering faded. I slowly but surely eased us into the hard shoulder and after another inspection I removed the sock from the tank with the help of two pens and Minagh, who had been promoted to assistant mechanic while the other three awkwardly hung around without a clue what to do. After several unsuccessful attempts to restart the engine it became clear that we were going to have to abandon ship on the M1.

Late at night, we sat on the side of the road with Cavan bags on the ground beside us. My father didn't take the call well, or the news that he would have to arrange to have the car picked up the following day. The fact we had won and had performed admirably did little to lighten his mood. The rest of us were just giddy about our performance and the campaign ahead. We had to get Padraig Dolan, our stats man, who was also heading for Dublin to double back down the motorway and rescue us as the team bus had returned to Cavan with most of the panel. The five of us got home at 1.30 a.m. and as we got in the door we just laughed at the things we did for Cavan football and the sacrifices we were so happy to make.

A lot of blood, sweat and tears had gone into getting our preparations right as this was the last chance for so many of us. We had serious talent in our ranks. I passionately believed that if our steady progress continued, we could give the Cavan senior team a new lease of life. I saw it every time I went down to training with the seniors that year as the backup to James Reilly, who was an experienced net-minder and twice nominated All-Star, but there just wasn't the same buzz to the senior group. I think the lack of success over the years had eaten into the group's spark and energy. It needed to be refreshed and I felt our bunch, who were so committed to chasing a dream together, were the ones to inject a new hunger and optimism into the team. While we all felt that connection to each other in abundance, we had to first prove we had what it took to become winners and put Ulster medals in our pockets.

3
The Journey

Sport always had the capacity to take me to a completely different place, helping me to leave the real world behind and bring me into that 'zone' experts often talk about. It was why I adored being a goalkeeper.

Back then, it enabled me to be the person I thought I was, in an exciting environment. I didn't have to worry about normal pressures like making friends, what other people thought about me or school grades. It felt like a carefree and non-pressurised situation that enabled me to thrive. It brought me social standing and respect in a way I had never experienced before. I could let all other aspects of my life fall away, and just give myself over to the game, to the part I had to play to help our team win. It was a feeling I associated with being a Gaelic footballer, but the first time I felt that buzz, that clarity, wasn't on a Gaelic football field.

I lived in Donaghmede in Dublin until I was 11. Gaelic football wasn't that big in my family; soccer was my first sport. I wasn't a natural, to put it mildly. On one occasion, instead of running around trying to get the ball like the rest of the kids, I was on my hunkers in the middle of the field with my socks pulled up as high as they would go and my jersey pulled down below them, trying to keep warm. Cold and completely uninterested in the game, I will never know how I was even left on the pitch during one of my first matches. If chance hadn't intervened, I don't think I would have lasted too long playing competitive sport. But later that season, our regular goalkeeper didn't show up for a game against local rivals Baldoyle.

'Who wants to go in goals today?' asked my Trinity manager Brian Sheehan. It was like a teacher asking a group of kids to show their homework: everyone muttered to themselves, 'Please don't pick me'.

I put my hand up. 'I'll do it.'

The applause from the sidelines and the praise from my teammates for the saves I made that day made me feel like I had never felt before. I had found a calling in life, and I became fascinated by it. I was hooked.

At nine years of age, I was sent to play for one of the better schoolboy clubs in Ireland, Belvedere FC, and that is where I really honed my skills. I felt like I became a different person in goals. Quiet in the classroom and at home, I confidently barked orders at those on the field, the way I had been coached.

Rather than running around the pitch like the rest of them, I could study the game like a science, and I came to excel at it. It was still all very much soccer at that time, my passion for GAA was only uncovered when we moved to Cavan.

As I stood in the changing rooms of Brewster Park getting ready to don the Cavan shirt in the match against Fermanagh, I was never more desperate to win a game of football or more focused on executing my role as a goalkeeper perfectly. Without realising it, this campaign had consumed my life instead of supplementing it. 16 March 2011 was the day. I had thought about little else since waking up in that hospital bed in November wincing in pain, my mind primed to get myself ready to play in the first round of the Ulster under-21 championship. Relationship problems were put to the back of my mind, and college commitments were knocked down my list of priorities. Going out at night and being a normal student like most of my friends seemed such a mundane existence. There wasn't a day that I didn't think about playing for Cavan. I was obsessed with it, and by thoughts of our team succeeding.

After months of waiting, we were about to play Fermanagh in the first game of our Ulster campaign. The pre-match meeting in the Meadow View Inn was relaxed, and we were ready for action. Terry talked us through various bits and pieces, while Anthony Forde used video clips from earlier games that season to show us the things we'd done well when we focused and performed as one. I thought of my saves against Meath a month earlier and it was a timely reminder of how far I had come and what I had been through to earn my spot in the match against Fermanagh. My mind was fully focused and I was excited about the challenge ahead – anything else going on in my life just faded into the background.

On the bus to the match a few of the boys had iPods in their ears but most sat back and sipped water or Lucozade as we watched *A Year Til Sunday* on DVD – the classic fly-on-the-wall documentary on Galway's senior All-Ireland football triumph in 1998. Before I knew it we were coming into Enniskillen and the DVD changed from the Galway footballers back to the reel highlighting our successes over the year and what our whole team and style of football was about. The clips clearly showed our work rate, tackles, desire, creativity in attack and our support play all over the field. We knew we would need to get all those things spot on to book our place in the last four of the province as Fermanagh had quality performers such as Tomás Corrigan, Sean Quigley and Ryan Jones.

Standing in the dressing room before the game, I just knew we weren't going to lose. 'All right, lads, let's get ready to put on the jerseys. We'll put them on together, just like we've done everything together all year,' said Terry.

I took my jersey off the hook behind where I sat and I felt an energy flow from the fabric into my skin.

I immediately turned it around in my hand to look at the number I had worked so hard to make my own. I was wearing number one again. At that moment I didn't care about anything else. I looked around at my fellow troops getting ready to suit up. I felt like a Power Ranger, my uniform about to transform me from a normal person into a larger-than-life character, ready to defeat my opponent. It was my first championship game for Cavan in two years and my determination to emerge victorious was greater than ever before. I looked at the faces of my fellow Breffni warriors and I knew they craved it too.

In the second half, as Fermanagh hunted for the goals they needed to get back into the game, I proved my worth to the team. They had a free out around the 45-metre line and I called Gearoid in with me on the line as extra cover. 'Anything drops short, you contest it and I'll cover behind you as always, all right?' I said.

'Yeah,' was all I got as he nodded his head and tried to catch his breath.

The free was dropping short outside the edge of the square. 'Up you go, G,' I called.

He went to attack the ball but as he rose, the Fermanagh forward flicked it goalwards. Before I knew what was happening, my hands were rising. They connected with the ball and pushed it up into the air. The momentum carried me to the ground, but as fast as I went down, I bounced back up twice as quickly to field the looping ball again and clear our lines.

'Thatta boy, young O'Mara,' I heard a voice shout from the stand after I had off-loaded possession. But the silent pat on the head from Gearoid before he galloped back out the field meant much more. We went on to win 1-13 to 1-7. Considering I had invested so much time and energy into that one contest, there was a terrific mixture of relief and excitement at the final whistle.

There was little time to dwell on it though, as we were scheduled to play the Ulster semi-final just seven days later. Off the field, I was living week to week; a simple process of eat, sleep, play, repeat.

For the second year in a row, we were due to meet a Jim McGuinness team that was busy perfecting a system that had already yielded an Ulster title at this level and one All-Ireland under-21 final appearance – the system that would ultimately take Sam Maguire to the hills of Donegal in 2012.

Before the game, we lost Niall Murray in the warm-up through illness. He hadn't been feeling well in the days leading up to the contest but he was every bit as invested in our team succeeding as the rest of us. When most would have gone out and tried to start, he held up his hand and admitted he wasn't fit to do his job and handed that task to someone else. It's the sort of responsible and selfless person he is.

As we prepared to leave the changing room, I saw Niall leaning against the wall in the corner. I'm not sure how many others saw him cowering there with his head in his hands, but I felt I owed him another day out.

Our management team got our tactics spot on, and the boys performed to perfection. To beat the defensive system Jim had created, our half-back line was told not to go past the halfway line. We were looking for swift and early balls straight into our full-forward line when they were on, and if things became too congested then patience was to be our motto. The players were being trusted to make the right call on when to push and when to hold.

Many times during that game against Donegal when all avenues were blocked by the yellow wall, we calmly recycled the ball back out to our spare bodies in defence who had refused to follow their men into the danger zone. From there, we went at it again – simply probing for an opening, and with the quality and intelligence of the forwards we had, the openings came. When we were turned over in possession, it also meant that we frequently had six defenders in place and wouldn't succumb to the ruthless attempts at counter-attack that McGuinness so desperately wanted to work.

Our team had been presented with a problem, and as a group we had studied it, broken it down and solved it. It brought a different type of satisfaction than totting up a big score – more like a game of chess. I've never played on a team before or since that worked so thoroughly to overcome a system.

From the second the ball was thrown in, I thought about nothing but the puzzle laid out in front of me.

I respected the system that McGuinness had introduced. It often meant his team ended up with 14 players behind the ball, but it also demanded more from Gaelic footballers physically. While a strong defence was clearly his main priority with all the additional bodies, the system still just couldn't muster the scores needed to secure victory without lung-bursting runs up the field from players to break out of their defensive formation. The Glenties man took the fitness required to play the game to new levels. It asked plenty of questions of us as players too and we had to think on our feet. It definitely made us a better, smarter and more complete team.

Late on in the game, defending champions Donegal came looking for a goal, with Patrick McBrearty to the fore. There was a massive goalmouth scramble after my save from the initial shot trickled clear across the small square. My first reaction was to pounce like a cat and smother the rebound with both hands. Lying on the ground, facing my own goal and surrounded by Donegal men desperate to score, I looked up. There were Darragh Tighe and Oisin Minagh in the goalmouth covering me as I crawled, frantically trying to get the ball out of the danger zone.

When I say that football had the capacity to take me to another place, I mean that, in moments like these, my mind was at peace – there was no internal dialogue. A split second would feel like a minute, and in that moment I felt a mental, even spiritual, connection with the lads, even though we were surrounded by thousands of screaming supporters and a handful of Donegal men trying to impose themselves on us. I was just there, in that very moment. This was why I was so happy to let football consume me the way it did; for those little moments of magic that offered a satisfying sense of escape.

After getting back on my feet and riding a few hefty shoulders, I stood on my line and shouted at all those in blue in front of me, 'Last few minutes. Finish strong, boys. No goals. No fucking goals.' The hairs stood up on the back of my neck.

I will always remember the sight of my two teammates lurking behind me, sweeping in on the goal line to help prevent a goal if I lost control of the ball. Those men are and always will be legends in my mind and were major factors in us advancing to the provincial decider against Tyrone on a scoreline of 0-12 to 1-4.

For the first time in my life, I was playing in an Ulster final. All we had to do was work our socks off for one hour of our lives – 3,600 seconds. I couldn't have picked a better team to take on for what was the biggest game of my life. The Tyrone outfit, featuring the likes of Peter Harte, Matthew Donnelly and Niall Morgan, were the one side we could never beat when we were younger. At under-16 they had hammered us. At minor they had absolutely crushed our hearts as our naivety cost us dear in Clones when we were on the brink of a provincial decider.

For years, the idea of securing an Ulster title had brought serious drive and focus to my life and I was desperate to do it. As the big occasion loomed, I was reminded of all the heartbreak and agony over the years. It was crazy to think about how long I had been working towards becoming a champion. In 2007, when I was just 16 and starting my first minor championship game for Cavan, we lost the first round to Down, and eight months of training went down the drain just like that, as there was no backdoor or second chances at the level. In 2008, we got a three-game run to the Ulster minor semi-final under the guidance of Mickey Graham and Paul McCorry but eventually lost out to this Tyrone team. In 2009, I went straight into the under-21 side that was beaten in the first round by an Armagh outfit inspired by Jamie Clarke, and the following year I had been sidelined as the team lost the final to Donegal.

This was the year that the hurt and agony had to stop. We were chomping at the bit as the ball was thrown in. Gearoid McKiernan grabbed it and banged it inside. Niall Murray, back from his disappointment in the previous encounter, raced onto it and stuck it in the net after 11 seconds. We took control in the first minute and never relinquished it.

It was an unbelievable game and I have never seen the intensity we brought that night matched by any other team I was involved in. We didn't give them an inch. Damien Barkey collided with a Tyrone player in the second half and knocked him into next week with the force of his shoulder. It was big truck, little truck, smash. It was a completely fair hit but it forced the attacker to wave the white flag and be replaced. As he was being carried off, Barkey was in front of the goals and ready for the next play. I clearly wasn't the only man possessed. Again I felt the connection between us.

To win an Ulster title with that group was incredible. Seeing Darragh Tighe jump up and down like he did at the sound of the full-time whistle made all the effort and energy put in over the years worthwhile. Hearing the Cavan supporters roar with pride and excitement when the game was in the final minutes is something I will never forget. The hair stands up on the back of my neck thinking about the pride and passion the people of Cavan have for football.

Handing them an Ulster crown meant a lot. It was the first at under-21 level since 1996 and the first of any kind since 1997. I got to stand on the pitch and look at my good friend Gearoid McKiernan raise the cup over his head to deafening roars and rousing applause. When given the microphone, the first people he thanked were the supporters who had fuelled the honesty, passion and enthusiasm of our team and helped to drive us over the finish line. 'I'd like to thank the Cavan supporters for being great throughout the whole year. They haven't had much to cheer about over the last couple of years . . . This year is for you as much as it is for us.'

We had done it. We had bucked the trend. We changed Cavan football for the better like we said we would. A month earlier I had promised several players that we would celebrate all night when we had our medals in our pockets, but that wasn't to be. The Croke Park fixture-makers in their wisdom had put us down to play against Wexford in the All-Ireland semi-final just three days later. So as a group we went to the swimming pool in the Slieve Russell after the game and were still in there that night at 12 o'clock, fully focused on chasing All-Ireland glory.

When I woke the next day I thought of one simple thing, and it felt sensational: the class of 2011 had delivered. I was an Ulster champion.

4

The Fall

I am an Ulster champion. I am an Ulster champion, I told myself again. I knew I should be confident.

I knew I should have felt privileged to win a provincial title, but, after the initial high, I didn't. I knew I should have felt relieved and accomplished to have overcome my injuries to achieve my long-held goal, but I didn't. I didn't feel good at all.

After the conclusion of the under-21 campaign in May 2011, my commitment to football started to disintegrate at an alarming rate. An early sign of this came with the senior team, with our Ulster championship campaign just around the corner. The seniors had a match against Carlow on a Friday evening in late May, as well as training on the Saturday and Sunday. A problem arose as a number of the under-21s who had been called up to the senior squad had booked tickets months earlier to see Kings of Leon perform in Slane on Saturday 28th. It had been all planned midway through the under-21 campaign when we promised ourselves that we would have a blow-out together after winning the provincial title.

Terry wasn't happy with our plans and felt it sent out the wrong message to the senior team, which had just been forced to accept ten rookies into its ranks. The panel had gone through significant change and only 13 players had remained from the championship panel chosen by Tommy Carr the previous year. Terry was probably right, given it was a few weeks before we opened our senior championship campaign against Donegal, but as far as I was concerned we had given Terry Hyland and Cavan football 100 per cent of our lives for the previous seven months and all we were asking for was to be excused from one training session – not the entire weekend. We vowed that we would be there on Sunday morning for training, but stood our ground about skipping the Saturday, despite his protests.

When we turned up on the Sunday there was a strange atmosphere. We trained away as if nothing happened – until the end, when those of us who had gone AWOL were called out and told we were in for some punishment. I had to stand in the goals and touch one post, only to have a ball fired at the other side of the goals. We did it 50 times in a row – unlike any training exercise, it was designed to hurt. It might not sound like it, but trust me, if the fittest player in Ireland did that drill he would be gasping for breath from the explosive power required to spring across the goal, get back on his feet immediately and do it all again. It was energy-sapping stuff.

I was sitting on the ground, my lungs burning, when Val Andrews, the senior manager, strolled over to me with a smile on his face. 'Well? Was it worth it?'

'Absolutely,' I said as I strolled off towards the changing rooms in Kingspan Breffni Park singing Kings of Leon songs to myself. Looking back, I am amazed how my relationship with the game had changed so drastically and how incidents like this failed to ring alarm bells in my head.

~

The 2011 summer campaign with the Cavan senior team was a short one. I knew we weren't moving well, but we learned the hard way just how far off the mark we were. Donegal wiped the floor with us in Ulster on a scoreline of 2-14 to 1-08 with Paddy McBrearty, still a minor at that stage, leading the way with 1-03.

The season went from bad to worse as Longford tanked us at home by 11 points in the first round of the qualifiers to put the senior team out of its misery. I had grown weary of the constant travelling up and down from Dublin. I remember sitting in the dressing room and looking around me wondering if this was it, if this was what I would have to put up with for the rest of my football career. It was sheer and utter mediocrity and the polar opposite of the team from which I had just graduated.

My last memory of that campaign was sitting in a Cavan pub after the Longford humiliation and listening to a man slag off the team to Niall Murray and me when the result came up on the RTÉ news bulletin. He hadn't a clue who we were as we sat there quietly sipping our pints, or how much we had sacrificed for Cavan football. It was clear that my relationship with football was already in decline by the end of that campaign under the guidance of Val Andrews.

In need of a new distraction, I was thankful that I was working for the second summer in a row in the GAA Communications Department in Croke Park. It was fantastic to see how the association worked behind the scenes. I was part of a brilliant team that consisted of Lisa Clancy, Director of Communications, Alan Milton, Head of Media Relations, as well as my two other musketeers, Cavan woman Siobhan Brady and Gary Finn, who hailed from Roscommon, as he was always quick to point out. They were fantastic to work with and we had some great laughs together.

The best thing about work was that it gave me responsibility and accountability. I had to be in by a certain time, and when I was there I would create a to-do list that gave me an automatic sense of satisfaction as I ticked jobs off and went about my days. So while other areas of my life felt like they were growing out of my control, my job was the one thing I could rely on. Things really started to spiral, however, when that work came to an end and I went back to DIT in September 2011 to complete the last year of my journalism degree. Night after night since I had finished up working in Croke Park and returned to college at the end of the summer, I lay in bed staring at the ceiling, questioning my existence.

I questioned the GAA too, and I wondered why I gave it the commitment I did. My drive and focus had left me. My weekly dose of adrenaline and satisfaction was gone. Playing football used to make me feel ten feet tall but that all seemed a distant memory. I began to dread the sport I once adored; my injury niggles had returned and the game was no longer coming close to bringing out the same buzz that it had during our Ulster campaign just months earlier. The suffering didn't match the reward. And with that gone, my life felt pointless.

That winter saw me lying in bed in Dublin, hiding from the world with nothing but my own conflicting, torturous thoughts for company. I would try to distract myself by reading or watching television or films online. I would lie there feeling worthless, with no energy, questioning my existence. When I remembered the person I used to be, I felt worse. I would see the broad smile on my face showing the perfect teeth that had taken three years of braces to achieve. I would see myself interacting with those around me. I'd visualise myself lying content beside my girlfriend on the couch in a world of our own, as I had done the previous year, and I realised that I was so much happier before our relationship ended. Then I'd be standing in the middle of a packed stadium, commanding the other players around me, emitting calm and confidence. I wished I could still get lost in the moment in that good kind of way. Guilt swept through my veins whenever I recalled that previous version of Alan O'Mara.

I slumped in my bedroom each day, repeating the process over and over again. I had yet to fully realise that I was trapped under a cloud of depression and life was passing me by. I felt like I was the only person in the world who was struggling, because every single fibre of my being made me feel isolated and lonely. Nothing seemed worthwhile in my life, not even the effort required to wash, shave or make something to eat. Even getting up to go to the toilet became a problem.

It often took the realisation that I was about to empty my bladder on the mattress to spark me into life. As I stood over the bowl after my scramble to get there, it would dawn on me just how pitiful I had become and it gave me another excuse to loathe myself. Everything seemed irrelevant, even this most basic act.

Being a goalkeeper, many people presumed that I wasn't fast or agile enough a runner to be an outfield player, but in my prime I was the third fastest on the Cavan team over five metres and fourth fastest over 20 metres. I'd always been nimble on my feet, but now I could barely walk to the bathroom, I felt so drained.

For a while the only thing I enjoyed was drinking, but then the nature of my hangovers began to change.

Sometimes I would get drunk again the next day to get rid of them, and to provide temporary respite from the dark mood I found myself in. But then, one night when I was drunk, the two voices in my head debated whether I should live or die – it was almost like an out-of-body experience. I was there, but I wasn't. I was just a passenger, listening to this conversation ensuing about how pointless my life had become. It was temporary insanity. I found it degrading, confusing and traumatising to be assessing my life's worth like that, upset and alone. I was regularly questioning myself and was constantly thinking about love, my family, work, college and how it bored me, and my life in general. What was the actual point of my existence? It was a constant loop of one step forward, two steps back as I edged closer and closer to the abyss.

When I woke in the mornings I ate whatever was within arm's reach and stayed in bed for hours with only my laptop for company. I survived on packets of Skips, wine gums and the share-size Aero bars that I had stockpiled to keep me going during my hours of binge-watching the likes of *Game of Thrones* and *The West Wing*.

I told myself that I could skip the first week of the semester after working so hard all summer, but one week became two and things snowballed from there. To say that my lecturers rarely saw me in Aungier Street would be putting it mildly. I turned my focus to regular escapades in Dublin's nightclubs.

The alcohol began to affect my train of thought. Normally a feed of drink would have brought a sudden high that would lull me into a false sense of happiness, but that had changed. One night I found myself sitting on the lid of a toilet in Copper Face Jacks, hiding from the world. I had been standing on the edge of the dance floor when all of a sudden I became paranoid. I felt like everybody in the place was looking at me. It was a surreal sensation, one that I had never experienced before, and, thankfully, haven't since. It was a borderline panic attack, and anxiety wreaked havoc on my mind and body.

As I sat there, slumped on the lid of the bowl with the door locked, laughter and conversation rang in my ears from the outside. My eyes filled with tears and my head with negative, self-conscious thoughts. I was trying not to cry. I took out my phone and started to type deep and disturbing thoughts into the 'notes' section to remind myself the next day of what I had endured.

~

Three days after Christmas in 2011 I was gazing at the flickering flame in the fireplace at my family home. It was comforting. I could feel the heat rising out of the fire and spreading across my face. I looked at our decorated tree, some of the gifts I had, and the endless food nearby and I told myself that I didn't want to go to a two-day training camp with the DIT team. I had no interest in playing in the Sigerson Cup, despite it being the pinnacle of college football.

The sinister voice in my head told me to stay right where I was. It told me I hated football. Football was the Grinch to my Christmas, but as I sat on the couch mulling over whether to go, a second, more reasoned voice in my head, reminded me that I was obliged to be there because I was a sports scholar. I trusted its wisdom and forced myself off the couch, packed my bag full of waterproof gear, boots, gloves and towels and got into my car.

The pitch we were slogging away on that night was barely lit. We relied on the floodlights from the Astroturf running perpendicular behind the goals to light up the area where we were working. I was standing in the middle of a puddle and although I was there in body, I didn't feel there in mind or spirit. The feeble light flickering its way through the net and railings reminded me of the warm, comforting fire at home.

I was wondering why football was not enjoyable to me anymore. I couldn't understand why it was no longer giving me the emotional highs I had become so reliant on. I missed being part of the Cavan under-21 team too, and that was made worse by the fact that our team was finished as a collective. Some of us would go on to play for the Cavan seniors but that team would never truly be a unit again as many of us were now too old to play underage football. I missed the sense of togetherness and understanding we had. Never before had a team ever given me such a strong sense of belonging.

Surrounded by DIT teammates, that little voice whispered in my ear again, asking me what the hell I was doing there. It told me I was conning my teammates and that I was a fraud. *You aren't the keeper you were and you don't deserve a scholarship. You should have stayed at home.* This conversation had played in my head so many times in previous months but I had yet to find the answers to my questions. I continued to plod along, coasting rather than excelling like I had done so passionately and vibrantly on the field.

After training I stayed with Gearoid McKiernan in his house, as the house in Drumcondra where I was now living was completely empty. My family and friends were at home enjoying their Christmas while I was being a slave to another GAA master. Having worked as a selector with Paul Clancy with the DIT fresher team that won an All-Ireland in 2010, Paul was now my manager. Part of me felt that I should have been giving him more than I was, but the reality was that I wasn't sure what I had left to give. I felt so empty and drained all the time.

I was doused in negativity. It was manipulating my thoughts, and that night I spent my time moaning about a sport I had always adored. I was completely and utterly disillusioned with football and blamed it for everything that was wrong in my life. I often wonder what type of person Gearoid saw that night, when just months earlier we had gone on the journey of a lifetime together. We'd overcome Fermanagh, Donegal and Tyrone so he could become the first Cavan man in 14 years to hoist a cup aloft in front of the Breffni faithful.

Eventually, blitzed by all my pessimism, mixed with some recollection of fond old memories of playing football together for Cavan and DIT, we decided it was time to hit the hay because we had a challenge match the following day. After he showed me to the guest room, he went into his own bedroom and shut the door, and I presume he nodded off to sleep like any normal person. I, on the other hand, took a sleeping tablet, but even that didn't knock me out.

I was taking sleeping tablets and I still couldn't sleep. I mean, what the hell was wrong with me? I stayed up reading Olympic boxer Kenny Egan's book in the hope that that might distract the whispers in my head enough to enable me to nod off. Instead, it made me ask myself even more questions. I read about Egan's extreme high of achieving Olympic success, something he had worked towards for years, and its immediate aftermath, which felt somehow devoid of meaning. He had turned to alcohol as a way of coping with his disillusionment. It all seemed eerily familiar.

Exhaustion gradually overcame me, and as my eyes grew heavy I turned off the bedside lamp. It was a complete waste of time, however, as thought after thought raced around my head. After switching to my iPod I eventually dozed off but by 7 a.m. I was wide awake again. Altogether I'd had just three hours' sleep. That voice was talking to me once more, asking why I didn't just stay at home and avoid football. I wondered if I was going mad. Was this how insanity felt?

Desperate for a distraction of any kind, I glanced around the room to see if there was a television, but there wasn't. My head fell back into the pillows. I lay there staring at an unfamiliar ceiling – questioning and wondering about everything in my life. Football was at the forefront of the debate but I was also thinking about my prolonged struggle with injuries, the death of my grandfather the previous November, breaking up with my long-term girlfriend, and first true love, late in 2010, surviving financially as a student and everything that went with it. I was analysing my life to try and make sense of why I felt the way I did.

The voice in my head on that morning focused on how every game I had played since losing the All-Ireland U-21s, the biggest game of my career, seemed a massive anti-climax. It told me football was the reason for my unhappiness. That march to the final in Croke Park, the brilliant adventure with a special bunch of players, was a lifetime ago to me.

I thought of our All-Ireland under-21 semi-final victory just three days after that memorable triumph over Tyrone. I remembered how exhausted we were and how our spirit and sheer determination got us over the line. I remembered how well I played in Parnell Park, how I had stepped up when my team needed me most in the second half, to thwart Wexford on two occasions and keep us ahead. I visualised Niall McDermott and young Jack Brady leading the attack, how the latter went from being a young lad on the team (just 18) to a real leader, a baby-faced assassin. I saw Fergal Flanagan making a double save on our goal line after a Wexford forward rounded me and looked certain to score. I saw the exhaustion on Kevin Meehan's face when I roared at him during the second half that we needed to up our game. We stretched every sinew we had. If the Ulster win over Tyrone was about intensity, that semi-final victory was definitely about resilience. We were boys who had to become men, and we had loved every second of it.

Next up was the trip to Croke Park and the chance we'd had to become All-Ireland champions. Normally the under-21 final is played in a ground situated between the two competing counties, but with the Cavan faithful fully behind the team and desperate for success at national level, it was agreed that our decider would be the curtain-raiser to the hurling league final between Kilkenny and Tipperary at GAA HQ.

It felt like destiny: the boys from Cavan going to Croke Park and sealing the deal – to become heroes for their county. It turned out to be a day I will never forget, that much is for sure, but for all the wrong reasons. There was no doubt the occasion got to some of our team and we never got close to bringing the intensity we showed against Tyrone. We were outgunned and outclassed by a vibrant and classy Galway team on a scoreline of 2-16 to 1-9.

After 14 minutes we were only down 0-4 to 0-3 but it all went wrong after that, and by half-time we were 11 points behind. For one of the goals, I made the best save I can ever recall but they scored from the third rebound of the same play. It just wasn't our day. Midfielder Tom Flynn's shot was deflected by Damien Barkey, and despite my body going to the left, I managed to get my right hand back to it to deflect it onto the crossbar. The ball was kept in play by the Galway corner-forward and they eventually scored. As the Galway forwards wheeled away in celebration, I was on my hands and knees under the Davin Stand cursing, in complete disbelief that they had managed to get the ball past me when I had felt so invincible coming in to the game.

That loss in Croke Park was like being taken to Disneyland as a child and being allowed to go on the most dangerous and thrilling ride, only to be told after just one go that I'd have to stay on the bumper cars from then on. I was lucky enough to have experienced that rush, an extreme high, and I thought nothing else could ever compare.

Now, in late-December 2011, as New Year's Eve approached, I lay in Gearoid's house, and thought about the fact that, in the months since that match, nothing had matched the feelings I'd had playing on that team despite transitioning to the Cavan senior squad on a full-time basis. Maybe I was too emotionally attached to the team; maybe I invested too much energy, physically and mentally. It had been the first thing I thought of when I woke up and the last thing that crossed my mind before I went to sleep, and often I'd even dream about it.

All of a sudden the conversation in my head was interrupted by Gearoid knocking on the bedroom door to wake me up for a game on a miserable winter morning. Little did he know.

When I was younger, all I had wanted to do was play sport. I spent my days jumping and diving on the concrete paths outside the house. When my parents would call me to come in for the evening, I'd jump around after a sponge ball on the beds, couches, and across the carpets and the wooden floors. I would commentate away to myself, always so happy in my own little world. Back then the voice in my head was a far more innocent and positive companion; we would dream of stopping goals in big stadiums some day. I was going to be the best in the world; the next Oliver Kahn or Peter Schmeichel. I was sure that my calling in life was to keep clean sheets. I simply loved how it made me feel.

But the challenge game that December morning couldn't have been further from that inspiring place I'd imagined in my childhood. All I remember was looking at the deteriorated surface around me and wishing that a hole would open up and swallow me. I even visualised an alien spaceship hovering over the field and zapping me away – anything to get me out of the living hell I'd found myself in.

I'd left Gearoid's house to play NUI Galway, but I don't remember if we won or lost, or who was playing on my team. I do remember a shot going past me into the net, and how I lay on the ground, pressed face-first into the muck, wishing I could be anywhere else. I hated football. As I went to stand up and get the ball, I had an overwhelming urge to cry. I paused for a second and wondered if it was actually happening. In the heat of battle, I stood there in the middle of 29 other lads, an Ulster champion, a sports scholar, trying not to let tears run down my face. I pushed the feeling away and got the ball in my hands. I kicked it as long and as far as I could, but the feeling came right back. *This match is pointless. Why are you even here?*

I fought back and tried to care. I shouted at defenders and told them to go left or to drop off, but they were half-hearted calls. I didn't care about the game. I may have been fooling others but I couldn't con myself. I was as far from the exhilarating rollercoaster of that under-21 campaign as I had ever felt.

After a game of football on three hours' sleep I was driving home on the motorway. It was a soulless road, and a boring trip. The markings flashed by in a blur. I was simply staring into space and thinking about how I had just played the majority of a challenge match while fighting back tears. I asked myself what the hell was happening. Why did I feel the way I did? I told myself to pull it together, to snap out of it, but I couldn't change my train of thought. My morning continued to replay itself in my head as the road whizzed by in a monotonous blur. I hated myself for going to that training camp, when I could have just stayed at home by the fire.

There was nothing to distract me on the road home after the match, nothing to occupy my mind. The negative thoughts started to drown out the radio and I felt trapped in the car. I kept driving. I kept thinking. How had I got to this point? How had I reached the stage of being tempted to swerve my car into the concrete wall on the side of the motorway? Its greyness and solidity looked so appealing. How easy it would be just to veer into it and finish it all. I would never have to hear that voice in my head again, the one that now whispered: *Will anybody even care if you do it?*

The sudden visualisation of my parents at my funeral rescued me: looking at my mam and dad standing to the right of my coffin in our local church, my mam's head leaning on my dad's shoulder, bawling crying. A crowd of people standing behind her and my coffin.

I wound down the window and let the crisp air hit my face. I drove along like Scooby Doo with my head out the window and let the wind bounce off my skin. I was so numb on the inside. I just needed to feel something, anything. On I went like that down the motorway, oblivious to the other cars on either side of the road. I was lost in my own dark and confusing world. When I eventually got home, all I wanted to do was switch off. I was tired, cranky and I had accepted that I was depressed.

Weeks before, I had visited my GP, assuring myself that I would be fine if I could just get my sleep cycle back to normal. He had asked me if I was feeling suicidal, but I told him that while I was extremely low, I had never considered it. We agreed that sleeping would help my mood. But having got my sleeping tablets, read Kenny Egan's book, played through a game of football with tears in my eyes, had an hour-long conversation with myself in the car and had a moment where I considered ending my life, it finally sank in. At least that miserable drive had been good for something.

Like so many mothers, mine has that special talent for immediately sensing when something is wrong. So when I got home I was barely in the door when she asked, 'What's up with you, Alan?'

'Nothing,' I replied lifelessly.

She knew I hadn't been sleeping. I'd told her and Dad that I'd gone to the doctor for sleeping tablets, but right then, at that very moment, I was not myself. I was not the son they had raised and loved so much. I was a pale shadow of myself and she sensed that better than anybody else. She asked again. I tried to convince her I was just tired, but she knew I was lying. Mothers always know.

She stood over me on the couch while I lay there with headphones over my ears and my hood pulled up. I tried to pretend I was listening to them – even though there was no music playing – but she knew. 'Is everything all right with you?'

No reply.

'Are you feeling a bit depressed?' she asked. She stared at me and her eyes never left mine.

I couldn't ignore her any longer, but I had no clue what to say. An eerie silence filled the room. *Should I lie? What excuse could I give?* My mind tried to come up with something, anything, swirling faster than ever before. I had been put on the spot, and I was panicked by trying to disguise my feelings once again. I didn't know how to lie my way out of this one. Just like clockwork, the negative voice in my head piped up and urged me to keep it all to myself. Thankfully, it was swiftly overpowered on this occasion because I realised that I couldn't possibly feel any worse than I did in that moment. I swallowed the lump in my throat, held back the tears just long enough to cough up something that sounded like 'yes'.

She asked what was going on, what was getting me down. I didn't open up fully, I couldn't – I didn't understand what was happening to me, or why I felt the way I did. All I knew was that I couldn't go on this way anymore – dealing with the constant sense of emptiness and the lack of energy. The internal arguments were exhausting: my mind had just told me to kill myself when I knew I didn't want to.

Visualising myself in a coffin, seeing the hurt and pain it caused my family, was the final straw. I'd been having doubts for weeks, but now I was entirely sure that what I was going through wasn't normal.

Later that day, both my parents said they loved me and reassured me that I was going to get through this. My mam hugged me. We had our first real talk then about where I could turn for professional help, and we decided that the Gaelic Players Association should be my first point of contact.

With all that buzzing around my brain, I headed to my room to try to figure out how I had reached such a low point, how I could have suicidal feelings just six months after running out in Croke Park for the first time. I did plenty more thinking, questioning and wondering, but still didn't come up with any definitive answers.

5
The Room

There is no doubt in my mind that the first real step in my recovery process was admitting to my mother that I was not feeling okay that December day. By asking the question, she broke down so much of the fear that had prevented me from reaching out for help. It didn't have to be me who started the conversation; I didn't need to worry about how to rationalise it. I didn't have to explain it all to my parents in a way that made sense to me, or to them, which was important because the reality was that I was still incapable of doing that. All I knew was that I needed help. Thankfully, the woman who had brought me into the world 21 years earlier knew how to make it easy for me that evening: all I had to do was say 'yes'.

My mother asking me that question was such a pivotal moment in my life, because it was definitely the only time I answered it truthfully – but it dawned on me then that in fact it wasn't the first time somebody had asked.

One day I was lying in my house in Dublin, weeks before that torturous drive home to Cavan. Niall Kelly, a good friend with whom I had grown up playing football for Bailieborough Shamrocks, returned home from hours of lectures at college. He marched straight up the two flights of stairs to my bedroom and arrived with his navy bag still on his back. 'No college for you today, buddy?' he asked.

'Not at all, lad. Better things to be at than listening to some lecturer waffling on at me for hours,' I replied in the grumpy tone that had become so common from me.

He pushed on with the questions. 'Fair enough. Are you not getting up today, though, no?'

'I'm just chilling the beans, lad. You know yourself,' I said, pretending to look at my laptop again.

As he sat down at the end of the bed, I could feel him reaching out to me. I cringe now at how I shielded myself from his efforts, while he tried to draw me out of myself. I fobbed him off and told him I was grand, even though I hadn't got out of the bed all day – again. I really don't know how the alarm bells weren't already ringing violently with me, because they clearly were with the people who knew me best.

I lied and changed the subject. We went on to have one of those discussions where men say an awful lot without really saying anything at all. It was easier for me to deflect and fire a couple of questions his way, so we went with the usual nonsense.

'How'd you get on today?'

'Ah sure, the usual banter, lad.'

'Any women about the college?'

'Aye, few ones about all right. Saw that one you were with a couple of weeks ago.'

'Was she looking well?'

'A1, buddy.'

'Were you chatting to her at all?'

'Nope.'

'Fair enough. Out tonight?'

I think it was my lack of understanding of what I was going through that stopped me from reaching out to my good friend that day. After the conversation with Niall, I googled 'am I depressed?', but nothing I could find seemed to answer my question. Or maybe I just didn't find the reassurance I was looking for, as I landed on a random medical website that asked if I had experienced suicidal thoughts, a disturbed sleep pattern or if I lacked energy. I closed the tab.

Stuck in that confusing place, I just couldn't comprehend what was happening to me and why I felt the way I did. The spiral downwards continued. I felt rotten most of the time. I tried to ignore it all and trudge on with my unhappy life, hoping that football would start to make me feel good again, that I would get back together with my girlfriend, that drinking or staring at my laptop for hours on end would keep thoughts of my problems at bay, but the dark cloud didn't pass.

The truth was, in the run up to Christmas, I spent months contemplating the decision to reach out for help, but I didn't know what I needed help *for*. I knew something was off-balance within me, but what was it? How could I explain it to somebody else when I couldn't even explain it to myself? Was it all just a figment of my imagination? Was I just feeling sorry for myself? Did I just need to get up and get on with it like any strong man would? If I couldn't, did that make me weak?

Reaching out to the doctor before Christmas when I could no longer sleep had been the first step in my conceding that I could not deal with what I was going through, and the conversation with my mam opened up the discussion about seeking proper help.

The Gaelic Players Association had sent out a generic email to all its members in the build-up to Christmas 2011 letting players know that there was a 24/7 counselling service in place throughout the year should we ever need it. Having just played in an All-Ireland under-21 final six months previously and spent the summer on the Cavan senior panel, few people could have had any idea how much I needed to see that email.

Yet when I considered availing of help, I assured myself that it wasn't necessary; everything would be fine – even though there was hardly an ounce of joy in my life.

Twice during those winter months, I had sat alone in my shared house in Dublin with the number of the GPA helpline typed into my phone. When push came to shove, I just couldn't find the courage to tap the green button and take a step into the unknown. Who would be on the other end of the line? Would they think I was making a fuss over nothing?

The night after I'd come back up to Dublin with promises to my mother that I would get some help, I eventually made the call, I left my house and walked a few laps of the estate before successfully dialling the helpline. There was no way I could have had the conversation inside, in case one of the lads had overheard me. I wasn't ready to deal with any questions or the mortification I felt it would bring. After much procrastination I keyed in the number and fought the overwhelming urge to hang up as I waited for the mysterious person to answer. I was so paranoid that someone passing by on the street would hear me that when I saw someone walk towards me, I crossed to the other side of the road to make sure I stayed out of earshot.

Saying my name and county to identify myself as a player, and admitting over the phone that I needed to talk to someone, was unsettling. I was afraid I would be judged.

The fact that I was reaching out to a service that was exclusively for inter-county footballers and hurlers was certainly a bonus, but it had reached the stage where I knew I had to seek help from somewhere, and I didn't know where else to turn. I now know that both the Samaritans and Pieta House do incredible work in this area in Ireland.

As the anxiety and panic soared and that voice in my head urged me to get back to bed, the notion that I was calling a private and confidential service definitely helped me to hold strong.

'Hello. This is Alan O'Mara from Cavan and I am feeling a little bit . . . I think I need to . . . to talk to someone,' I said nervously. It was certainly not something I would ever have imagined myself saying in a million years. Just a year earlier, the very idea that I would be in this predicament would have been laughable to me. I had been so focused on getting fit and regaining my place on the under-21 team, so excited for the upcoming season – how could I possibly be depressed when I was busy chasing my dreams?

'No problem at all, Alan. There are a couple of options available to you. Are you based in Cavan, or are you working or in college elsewhere?'

I answered that I was studying in DIT.

'We have a counsellor working in a clinic in Drumcondra if that works for you?'

'That would be great. I'm actually living in Drumcondra myself, and I'd rather do it in person if I can,' I replied.

As it turned out I could have kicked a football from my house to the counsellor's practice, so if ever there were a sign for me to get out of bed and get some real help, that was it. I still smile to think of it; it was one hell of a coincidence, and what little encouragement it brought couldn't have come at a better time.

Despite the encouragement, on the day of my first appointment I was shaking with anxiety at the mere thought of opening up to a stranger. Part of me had wanted to reach out for help, and was glad I had. I knew I had to, but that other voice, the one that had suggested I crash into a wall, wanted me to wait for all my problems to go away by themselves. My inner debate continued to rage.

Having successfully made the short journey from my house to the clinic unseen by anyone who might recognise me, I was sitting in the waiting room when my anxiety returned at full force. My legs started to tremble and I forced my hands down on them out of fear that someone would notice my distress and ship me off to a mental institution in a straitjacket. Suddenly a wave of panic was urging me to get out of the room, back down the carpeted stairs and out the old Victorian door so I could run until there was no possible way anybody could ever associate me with this building or what it was for.

Just as I was about to stand up and escape, Niall, the GPA counsellor assigned to me, walked through the door, introduced himself with a firm handshake and calmly invited me to follow him into his room. When I entered I was taken aback. I had expected a leather chaise longue which I would lie on, close my eyes and tell this complete stranger about all my problems and why my life had become so terrible.

It felt surprisingly informal. There were just two cushioned, upright chairs in the room and a table in between – with a sandpit on top of it. I had no idea what that was for. Was he going to help me make sandcastles during our appointment? I cringed at the thought. I felt like a silly little boy on his first day of school, afraid to meet his new teacher. A large rectangular window filled the room with daylight, so the overhead light and the lamp in the corner remained switched off. It was soothing. It felt safe, and more importantly, private. I sat down and faced Niall, who had a notepad and pen resting on his lap. My legs started to tremble again ever so slightly and I had butterflies in my stomach. It hit me that I had absolutely no idea what I had signed myself up for. I was petrified, and now I was stuck here.

Jesus Christ, Alan. Why the hell have you come here? Are you mental? There he was – that other fella in my head running amuck again. There really was no escaping now.

Fuck me, what am I actually going to say to this fella? Like, what to say? Where to begin? I was sweating.

Niall assured me that all our chats would be confidential, which eased the waves of anxiety that were lapping through me. I'd had every intention of telling him that I hated football and that everything that was wrong in my life was its fault. I was angry at football, bitter towards it; there was no way it should have left me feeling the way I was, considering how much of myself I had given to the game over the years. A huge part of me had grown to despise it completely in a very short time. In less than six months I had gone from being a gladiator performing in an 82,300-seater stadium to trying not to cry during a match.

I felt better for a couple of hours after the first session, having got that rant off my chest, but I remained guarded about other areas of my life. I didn't go home straight away and wandered randomly through the surrounding area trying to clear my head. I was grateful that I had reached out for help and put myself in front of a professional, but when that satisfaction wore off, I was left with even more questions than before. Counselling sessions made me focus on the very things I wanted to forget, the stuff I tried to distract myself from by watching television or drinking. It seemed counter-intuitive, but in my gut I knew I had to give it a serious try. I couldn't just run away from the uncomfortable places the counselling sessions would take me to.

Over the following sessions, as we got to know each other and built a trusting relationship, Niall started to probe other areas of my life.

'Okay, so we've been talking a lot about football, but tell me what else has been going on? Are you working? In college? Are you in a relationship at the moment?'

'No, I'm not working at the minute. I'm in my final year of a journalism degree.'

'And how is that going?'

'Ah it's grand, but I'm not mad on it. I find it pretty boring. I thought about dropping out once or twice over the years but I said I'd stick at it and finish it out. I used to work in a newspaper back home, the *Cavan Post*, before I went to college. Being honest, I learned more in those 12 months than I would in ten years of studying.'

'What job did you have in the paper? What were you, 18 or 19?'

'I was 16 when I started but 17 for most of it.'

'You did your Leaving Cert at 16?'

'Yep.'

'That's pretty young. How come?'

'Well, I started school when I was, like, three, but turned four a few days afterwards. The playschool teacher told my mam that I needed to go to a proper school. I guess I must have chewed crayons better than the other kids,' I said with half a smile.

'And you never stayed back, or anything like that?'

'Nope, there was never any need. To be honest, I was always one of the smartest in the class even though I was younger than everyone else. My secondary school didn't have transition year at the time either, so I just went straight through and did the Leaving.'

'Good man. So tell me about the *Cavan Post*, then.

How did you end up there? What did they have you doing?'

'I'd got a summer job through Paul O'Dowd, who was training the Cavan goalkeepers and was the sports editor of the paper. It went well, so they offered me a job for a year as a sports reporter. I was actually meant to go to DCU to study business. The college were giving me a sports scholarship and all that, but literally the day before I was meant to move in to my place on campus, I realised I had no interest in doing that course, so I pulled out. I said I would work for the year before committing to anything.'

'That is a fine achievement, for someone straight out of school to get that job. So you just did that for the year?'

'Well, yes and no, I suppose.'

'How do you mean?'

'Well, for the first couple of months, yeah, I was just doing the sports reporter job, doing match reports and all that sort of stuff. But in December 2008 Paul left his role there. The fact it was so close to Christmas meant they found it hard to get a replacement, and they asked me to cover for a few weeks.'

'And how did that go?'

'I must have done all right because they came back a few weeks later and offered me the role of sports editor on a full-time basis.'

'And you are 17 at this stage?'

'Yep.'

'How did that feel at the time?'

'Great. I was really proud, and it meant I was earning good money too. I negotiated a pretty good salary.'

'Pretty impressive.'

'Yeah, I suppose it was,' I replied, and my mind wandered into the distance.

It clicked with me how I had grown up so quickly, and at 17, while most young people are either in school or college living a relatively carefree life, I was managing a pressurised job that meant I had to supply 26 pages of sports content to the good people of Cavan every week. I didn't regret it, as I learned a huge amount in that period, but Niall was getting me to think about myself and my past experiences in a very subtle way.

That's one of the first examples of how counselling helped me to lower my guard and start reflecting on events in my life. Starting out with subjects that were easier to discuss definitely helped to build up the trust between us and made for a great start, but I had a long way to go.

While I was happy enough to open up about that spell in my life, I still struggled to tell him about my break-up with a girl I'd been madly in love with since my teens. And I told him about the death of my grandfather, William, in a very matter-of-fact way, with very little detail – almost as if it hadn't been a big deal to me. As far as I was concerned, I was a man; this stuff happened in life and I needed to get on with it. I wasn't there to talk about those things, I wanted to focus on my relationship with football. My logic was that if I could fix that, the balance would be restored and my life would go back to how it used to be. I was certain that my frustrations and problems were somehow GAA-related and I told him so in no uncertain terms.

Over the weeks and sessions that followed during the spring of 2012, I began to see that there was more going on than a simple dislike of football. Working with Niall helped to slow down my thought process and put my head back together again; it was like arranging puzzle pieces. When I'd managed to start counselling, I was definitely looking for a quick fix, a miracle solution to my problems, but I soon learned that depression didn't work like that. In truth all I wanted – all I needed – was to be able to get out of bed in the morning and see the pleasure in my life again. That became my number one aim. I was no longer concerned about becoming the best goalkeeper in the country.

Counselling was a long, stormy process, though, and at times I wondered if opening up in this way was doing more harm than good – or whether it was doing any good at all. I would leave the session with a greater sense of hope and understanding, but within an hour or two the dark cloud would return to hang over my head until I met Niall again.

Often I struggled to sleep for days after our talks because I couldn't stop turning our conversations over and over in my mind, trying to make sense of it all. I was searching for the understanding that I so desperately craved. It was not easy to open up to someone the way I had with Niall, but eventually I began to regain some clarity and saw the very real benefits of the counselling.

I was trying to fight my way back, I really was, but this part of the journey was incredibly tough. I wish I could make it sound easy, but it was like cycling up a never-ending hill. So many times I just wanted to get down off the bike and sit on the ground in a huff at how unfair the challenge was. It sapped my energy, but I had to keep going if I wanted to arrive at the place of hope Niall helped me to see.

I wanted to rediscover my passion for life. There wasn't a miracle cure, I soon realised that, but Niall was there to help me on my way, to help me find my way out of the darkest places. Clearly he had experience that I didn't, and he could see the big picture in a way I simply couldn't from inside my depression.

Even though I was starting to understand much more about what I was going through, I didn't tell any of my friends that I was going to therapy. I felt compelled to hide it, to keep it a secret. I had so little energy, and most of whatever I did have was spent spinning a web of lies about where I was going, what I was doing and how I was feeling. I did tell my immediate family, however. They were fully supportive of my decision and wanted to be kept in the loop.

I know that when I began my treatment, the biggest mistake I made was that I thought I was just trying to beat depression in a one-off fight: Alan vs Depression. Twelve rounds. When I delivered what I believed was the knockout punch after months of perseverance and finally felt good again, I naively thought my fight was over. I felt that was it, and I could go back to living my life like before.

Somehow I think that approach fed the competitor in me for the better; it kept me going to the sessions. My hope was that eventually I could stand up in front of my family and say, 'I beat it. I'm back. Are you proud of me?' In my imagination I could see the sunshine and rainbows again.

Part of me could already hear the crowd roar after I made a save. As a strategy it made sense to me. Coming from a sporting background made it easy to buy into that mentality. I challenged myself to fight back against depression and get it out of myself. Niall warned me on several occasions against that reasoning, but I took no heed. Little did I know how right he was; you don't get a 'lifting the cup' moment with depression.

While I didn't always understand everything we discussed – things like talking through my emotions and how I processed them were alien to me – Niall encouraged me to be optimistic whenever we spoke and see things from a more balanced perspective. It was incredibly empowering and liberating to force my way, through counselling, out of the hideaway that depression encouraged me into. I will be forever grateful to the GPA for providing that service for me – free of charge – when I needed it most.

During the hours I spent in that room I learned so much about depression, and about myself in general. On the bad days, I learned to sense the dark cloud when it was coming. My head would feel physically heavy, I'd struggle to concentrate and my energy would dip while carrying out even the most mundane task. When I sank really low I suffered headaches that no amount of paracetamol could stop. They were at their worst in the morning and would tempt me to stay in bed. The counselling also made me much more aware of my relationship with alcohol, and I began to notice how much it affected my thinking for days after a binge.

I was proud that I was starting to gain a real understanding of my depression, but it was far from plain sailing. Although the depression was slowly lifting, I still hadn't fully accepted that it and counselling would be part of my life for the foreseeable future.

6
The Tears

Two or three times earlier that evening I swallowed hard and closed my eyes, waiting for the urge to pass. It was March 2012 and I had come home to Cavan for the weekend. The lump in my throat had come and gone over recent weeks, but this time it didn't seem to want to go anywhere. Something was different.

Thoughts were bouncing around my head at a frightening pace. We, my brain and I, had been doing this familiar dance for months – debating the validity of life. I felt like the Sméagol/Gollum creature from the *Lord of the Rings* series – two voices within one person, constantly arguing over everything, from what I should eat for lunch to whether my breathing was a waste of oxygen.

The waves of emotion kept churning so I said I was shattered and headed off to bed. I lay in the dark in the sanctuary of my room. Niall, whom I had been seeing on a fortnightly basis since January, had told me that this moment was going to arrive in the near future as part of my healing process.

'Lookit, Alan, don't be surprised if you get an urge to cry at some stage. How the body often heals after going through experiences like you have is through crying. As your depression lifts, your body will need to offload emotions that it has been carrying for a long time,' he said.

'Yeah . . . no bother,' I replied cautiously, not sure if I was ready to believe him or not.

I had left his office that day half-laughing to myself about the notion of breaking down in tears. I just couldn't see myself doing it. The last time I could remember crying properly had been when I had broken my arm in three places having punched the ground after conceding a last-minute goal during a school match. It was a goal that had lost us the game, and I had snapped. I put a few dents in the ground, and it did a number on me in return. Not one of my prouder moments, but it's a pretty clear indication of how much I cared about the game.

I had to get the position of it reset after the temporary cast had my arm set the wrong way in order to give it the best chance of knitting back together correctly. I let out some roars when they twisted it around hours later. Crying then seemed fair enough – the pain was incredible – but why would I cry over something going on in my head? It just didn't make sense to me, even though I'd been so close to tears so many times recently. Punching the ground to release my frustration hadn't done me any favours; maybe crying would help.

As I lay in bed I thought about all I had discussed with Niall during our sessions and played back the conversations in my head. I saw the jar he had drawn with his finger in the sandpit beside the desk. Something about the sandpit really caught my attention, and the image stayed with me. I could see the first line he traced towards the bottom of the jar – the point where a person's normal level of emotion was meant to be.

Then I noticed a second line, my level a few inches above it, worryingly close to the brim. That image really helped me to understand how depression was festering within me, and how it fed off all the things that had happened in my life. I thought they were my burden and mine alone to carry.

I thought of how the death of my grandfather, William, had inflicted a sense of loss that I had not experienced before. How I was lucky to know my other three grandparents, Pauline, Jan and Bill, so well and to see them on a regular basis. I was even blessed to have fond memories of three of my great-grandparents. I remembered helping the other men in my family to carry my grandfather's coffin up the aisle of the church and holding back my tears, trying to think of anything but him, despite the weight of his body and the wooden case pressing down on my shoulder. I kept telling myself to be strong for my mother, who had just lost her father, and that I couldn't cry in front of the packed church.

He was the first person whom I truly loved who passed away, and I didn't know how to deal with that bereavement. At the time of his death, while I hadn't realised it, the depression had had me almost completely numb, and I remember being disgusted at myself for not being as overwhelmingly upset as I felt I should have been. It made me feel cold and heartless, almost like a monster.

It was only months later when I began revisiting it with Niall that it really hit home. My grandfather was a wonderful, loving man. I thought of the good times we had shared together. We had known that his life in this world was coming to an end, so the family had gathered around to celebrate his 71st and, as it turned out, last birthday and his and my grandmother's 50th wedding anniversary. The last memory I have of my grandfather is quite fitting: he was sitting on the couch, fighting the urge to fall asleep but finding enough energy to be affectionate to his wife Pauline and to look around the room to smile at the family he had helped to build. He passed away a few days later, but that memory will stay with me forever. My grandparents loved each other with all of their hearts until the very end, and it made me think about how much I wanted a similarly long and fulfilling life too – despite the weight of the depression in my mind.

I thought again of how my heart was recently broken after a relationship ended. Despite my relatively young age at the time, I was truly in love with a very special girl, whom I was very glad to have in my life. We spent most of our formative years together, and we had a special bond. I always felt our relationship was far more meaningful than the short and sweet relationships that so many of our friends went through in spades at that age.

She was the only person I would even consider allowing to see me cry. I felt like I could let my guard down around her, that I could be honest about how I was feeling at any given time, about work, family and all the other inevitable stresses life throws up at different times. After the break-up I missed the emotional and mental outlet that our relationship had given me and felt a huge vacuum in my life. Whenever friends had asked me about that heartbreak, I had always just shrugged it off. 'How's the single life treating you?' was the inevitable question.

'Ah sure it's not so bad, lad. Shifting and drifting, like, you know yourself. Sure there are plenty more fish in the sea,' I would say.

Immediately after the break-up I felt certain that we would get back together at some point, but that only added to my confusion. There wasn't a day that went by without my thinking about her.

Initially a lot of the discussion with Niall revolved around my diminishing relationship with football and how I gradually sank deeper and deeper into depression after losing that All-Ireland under-21 final in Croke Park. We talked about my call-up to the senior team in 2011, and how after a few short weeks, I simply didn't want to be there. The sense of belonging and purpose I had felt with football had completely disintegrated despite Val Andrews and Terry Hyland calling up myself and nine others from the under-21s to the senior squad.

I had been doubling up all year as the under-21 goalkeeper and the senior sub-keeper to James Reilly when all of the other under-21s were left to focus on their own campaign. The atmosphere in the senior dressing room at that stage felt toxic to me and I often resented how I was the only under-21 that had to travel to league games with the seniors. That team had nothing like the chemistry I'd had during our under-21 campaign, and I didn't feel that same bond with those in the dressing room. The lads my age were my friends, my brothers, but the great majority of the senior squad were just teammates. I know that seems like reverse logic, but in my mind, be it right or wrong, the Ulster under-21 championship was my only goal, my true destiny, and everything after that was a distraction.

The senior team played away to Limerick in the National League in March 2011 and the team travelled down the night before to stay in a hotel. I had a slight niggle in my ankle, and I asked Terry to excuse me, but he insisted that the senior squad needed me as cover.

I knew what was more important to me when it came to choosing between the senior team or my hopes of winning an Ulster under-21 crown. I had gone to watch the senior team play for years as a supporter and they had consistently failed to make a mark in the Ulster championship. They had some good players, but they never seemed to get the chemistry right as a group; there was a high turnover of both players and management. I knew that wasn't going to change overnight, but I believed that the young talent coming down the conveyor belt could change everything.

After travelling to Limerick, we were fed early in the evening in the hotel and then left to our own devices. A gang of us gathered around a table playing cards, away from the eyes of the manager, but things took a turn for the worse when someone complained about being hungry, even though we'd only eaten together a few hours ago. Before we knew it, this stack of pizzas had been ordered. It was the night before a game. It was complete and utter madness. We spent most of the season getting our bodies into good shape, but the night before a game, the players were filling them with rubbish. It was just plain stupid.

As the only rookie in the squad at that stage, I wasn't prepared to make a stand – especially without the backup of my fellow under-21 players. Instead I took the easy option and ordered a box of chicken strips, laughed along with the rest of the group and got on with the cards. The last conversation I remember from that night was about where we were going to hide all the takeaway boxes so that Val Andrews wouldn't find them. We found a table with an overhanging tablecloth and the rest, as they say, is history. Limerick beat us the following day, 2-14 to 0-15.

Football and winning an Ulster title were no longer my main priorities in life. I was sick of investing my time and energy in an attempt to win a battle that the majority of people didn't even know was taking place.

As I lay in bed in my family home that March reflecting on it all, a tear broke through and trickled down my neck. That single drop was soon followed by another, which lingered somewhere between my lip and ear. I was flat on my back, trying to relax and stay calm. I felt like I wanted to cry. I knew I needed to. But for some reason I couldn't continue. I asked myself again if I was imagining it all. Was it all in my head? If the tears weren't coming like Niall had suggested, then maybe I just *thought* I was depressed. Had I been fooling myself over the past few months to give myself an excuse for losing my appetite to succeed in life? Gollum and Sméagol were at it again. They were relentless.

I searched for a distraction. My bedroom was dark. Night had descended but my eyes had adjusted to my surroundings. I could see my light-blue curtains and the outline of my television with a blue light shining to signify it was on standby. I wiped away the tear that was clinging to my cheek and presumed the worst of my peculiar mood was over.

Was that the best I could do? Then my eyes filled up again. This time I rolled onto my side and curled up into the foetal position. I pulled a pillow out from underneath my head and drew it close to my chest. At that moment I could feel the jar that Niall drew in the sandpit weeks earlier shatter in my gut.

Tears started flowing out of my eyes and rolled down my face like raindrops on a windowpane. The sensation as they touched my skin was unnatural. My stomach contracted as if more of my bottled-up emotions were being forced out of me drop by drop. Memory by memory and emotion by emotion, they climbed out.

I heard movement in the next room so I bit down on my duvet to smother the noise of my sobbing. I couldn't breathe anymore because I was so congested, worse than any cold or flu. My phone vibrated with a message but as I went to press the buttons, I trembled. My eyes blurred and I struggled to make out the text. I tossed the phone somewhere into the darkness and refocused my attention on my pillow. I stayed still and let it all come out. I switched to autopilot and let my body do whatever it wanted to do.

Deep inside me there was a place where I had chosen to contain years of emotions, feelings, memories, problems and thoughts. I could feel the weight of them physically dragging me down. Each time I had genuine worries about life I think I just forced my problems further down, locked them away and kept them to myself. I used football both as an escape and a distraction, but that relationship changed dramatically. My emotional jar had reached capacity. Stuff had been lingering in there, deep, deep down and away from the real world and real people for far too long.

The jar had reached breaking point and cracks had started to appear in the previous weeks and months. A little drop here and there gently hinted that I was fighting a losing battle, but I refused to give in. A few weeks previously, I had been cooking dinner in my house in Dublin alongside one of my friends when my eyes welled up with tears. I turned away from him and took a few silent, deep breaths. I forced the tears back down, out of sight, before I turned back around and continued the conversation. For the record, I wasn't cutting onions.

My stubbornness and ego ensured that the battle had lasted far longer than it needed to. I squeezed every bit of life I could out of that jar. A better man would have confronted these feelings a long time ago, but I scraped every last day, hour, minute and second I possibly could out of my emotional container.

Once or twice I thought I was done, wiped my face and blew my nose only for another wave to crash. About an hour after I entered my bedroom I lay my head on a wet and bogey-ridden pillow. Thankfully the breakthrough that Niall warned me about had come in my own bedroom where I had a private and important moment. There was no hysteria or drama; it was just me in the darkness doing what had to be done.

My little brother was in his own world watching a film just five feet and a partition wall away from me as I cried my eyes out, while my parents walked by my door and headed for their own bedroom. Nobody had a clue what was happening, and who could blame them? Who in their right mind would think that Alan O'Mara, an Ulster champion with Cavan and a sports scholar with DIT, someone who had spent years chasing a dream and finally achieved it, was at home clinging to his pillow for comfort on a Friday night as he sobbed his eyes out?

Before I trudged up the stairs to cry, I sat listening to Niall Quinn, the former Republic of Ireland striker, tell Ryan Tubridy about his experience with mental health after he retired and how the world of professional football reacted to Gary Speed's suicide in November 2011. At that time Speed was manager of the Wales international team and a former Premier League legend. His death made me more determined to build my resilience against depression but also caused me to worry about the future battles I was going to have with it. This wasn't measles; it could come back at any time.

Always a big soccer fan, I had idolised Quinn as a player when I was growing up, and I have fond memories of him leading the Ireland attack over the years. However, the reason I really respected and admired him dated back to 5 October 1999.

When I was just nine years of age my parents took my two brothers and me to the AUL grounds in Dublin where the Ireland senior soccer team were having an in-house practice match under the watchful eye of manager Mick McCarthy as they prepared for their upcoming Euro 2000 qualifier against Macedonia. I leaned against the fence and watched heroes of mine like Alan Kelly, Gary Kelly, Gary Breen, Denis Irwin, Steve Staunton, Niall Quinn and Robbie Keane go about their business and I was completely and utterly in awe. I was raging that Roy Keane and Ian Harte were absent from the squad, but getting to see Alan Kelly, Dean Kiely and Shay Given being put through their paces by goalkeeping coach Packie Bonner, another legend, was a surreal experience. I studied every move they made, determined that one day I would be as good as them.

Afterwards, as the players streamed out the gate that kept supporters a few yards off the field, my brothers David and Billy and myself desperately scrambled around hunting for autographs.

I had a piece of paper and got Niall Quinn, Mick McCarthy, Gary Breen and a few others to sign it. David had been given the responsibility of getting a brand new football that we'd bought on the way to the training signed by as many players as he could. However, his hunt proved less fruitful. As the players made a beeline for the bus, we followed them.

Standing at the entrance of the coach, my father Michael asked the security guard supervising the door if we could get the ball on the bus so the team could sign it for us.

'No balls on the bus,' he said forcefully.

'Ah come on, I have three young fellas here and it will make their day. Can you not pass it around while you're waiting for the rest of the team to get on? It won't take two minutes,' pleaded Dad.

'I said no balls on the bus.'

As he rudely repeated himself, Niall Quinn was just about to board when he turned on the spot and asked us what was going on. I presume he'd noticed the sharp tone of the bouncer's voice. As Dad explained, Quinn reached over and took the ball out of his hands. 'No problem. Hang on there for me,' he said as he disappeared into the bus with our shiny football and pen in hand.

A few minutes later he emerged, reached over the security guard's shoulder and said, 'There you go, fellas,' before returning to his teammates. Every player had signed the ball for us and to this day it sits on a shelf in my bedroom in Cavan. It was a simple gesture but one that we all greatly appreciated. And 12 years later, Quinn was about to help me again. This time, with his wise words to Ryan Tubridy.

'I walked out on football overnight really . . . I hit a six-month period where I literally wouldn't even answer the phone. I didn't want to know about people. I had my high and now I was experiencing a low.'

Tubridy then asked the Ireland legend to elaborate on the comments about his own depression, which he had made in the aftermath of Speed's passing. Until then, the Ireland striker had kept his struggles to himself.

'My comments were a direct response to the Players' Union, who decided that they had the answer, which was sending a booklet out to all the players. I know what I would have done with the booklet during the tough time that I faced . . . It said "this is how to overcome depression", and I felt that that wasn't good enough. I wish I knew three years before I finished playing football that there was going to be a drop, that there was going to be a low. It's over like a flash,' said Quinn.

Hearing those words from a man I had grown up worshipping made me think more about my own situation. I'm not sure if that interview with Quinn was my final trigger, or if it was going to a Cavan match for the first time in 2012 and standing on the terrace with my under-21 teammates Oisin Minagh and Darragh Tighe feeling completely detached from the team as they played Sligo under the lights of Cavan HQ.

As I lay in bed after that emotional off-load, I couldn't help but think about the darkest spell of my life and all that I had gone through over the previous months. I could see the light, though – and quite literally, as a ray of light meandered its way through the doorframe and into my line of vision.

I pulled the blanket tight and tried to sleep. I thought of the football a few feet away from me and thanked Niall Quinn for helping me finally accept that it was okay for an athlete to embrace his vulnerabilities.

7
The Return

As I finished my degree that May 2012, I had come through an intense period of counselling.

After we had gone our separate ways in late 2010, I got back together with my girlfriend during the spring of 2012. Although not officially an item for over a year, we had remained in sporadic contact as we never fully managed to break free of the pull we had on each other. After deciding to give it another go, the love, support, care and strength she gave me during one of the most confusing times of my life is something I will never forget. It was not easy for her to deal with my mood swings, and I'm not sure how I would have made it through that mentally draining period without her.

Despite the counselling, I was still very uneasy when it came to talking about my feelings with people, but for some reason it always felt different with her. Whenever we had meaningful conversations, I wasn't afraid to take off my mask. I knew she didn't fully understand my depression – sure, I barely understood it myself – but the important thing was that I never felt that she judged me when I opened up. She listened and cared. No matter how good, or indeed how bad, my mood, I nearly always felt better and happier in her company. I passionately and wholeheartedly adored her. I felt at ease when it was just the two of us together, and my inner debate tended to disappear altogether when I was around her. Without even knowing it, she had a special talent for getting me to live in the moment, rather than thinking about the past or worrying about the future. I would have given everything I owned to feel that way all the time.

During this time, I had somehow successfully finished my degree in Journalism at DIT, despite my deplorable attendance, and handed in my thesis, a study on how and why GAA inter-county players were using Twitter. Many of my classmates struggled to pick up work related to our degree, but by then I had already worked with the Communications team in GAA HQ, so that made things easier for me. A week after finishing my course I took up a full-time position with the GAA Communications Department in Croke Park as their National Social Media Coordinator – the same team I'd worked with during my two summers as an intern and whom I'd grown to know extremely well.

They knew what I could bring to the role, and I felt it was an opportunity far too good to turn down, even though I'd had offers to play football in Boston and San Francisco for the summer. When I'd started college, the job I'd just begun simply didn't exist, so it was great to find a place in the evolving media sphere. My friends couldn't believe I was getting paid to be on Facebook and Twitter all day on behalf of the GAA, but there was far more to it than that. Indeed, to anyone on the outside looking in I was flying high, but the depression was still gnawing at me and I couldn't figure out why. The battle had already seriously dented my self-confidence.

With an Ulster under-21 medal in my pocket that summer, I was one of many young Cavan footballers to be approached about playing football Stateside. The offers were never formal invitations; they would come in via a mutual friend on Facebook or by a phone call from a player who already knew he was heading out to a team. Promises of work and free accommodation for the three months spent over there were regularly used to strengthen the offer.

Part of me definitely wanted to travel, but I knew I still needed my family and friends near to help me cope with the low moods that were occurring sporadically.

In part, I resented my depression for putting me off visiting the US – I didn't feel strong enough to take a step into the unknown – but it meant a lot to be the person trusted to grow the GAA's presence online. It was to be my job to ensure that all 32 counties learned how to use social media, and it was a responsibility that I took very seriously. They had taken a punt on me as a recent graduate, but I'd like to think I justified their faith, as in the following 20 months the Association's direct social media following grew from 20,000 to over 180,000. I also worked with volunteer public relations officers at county level to quadruple the wider GAA community online to more than 800,000 followers.

Despite the amount of time I was putting in there, the Croke Park staff knew nothing about the depression that had been infiltrating my life, as I was still adamant that it remain a secret, afraid of the stigma that was attached to the diagnosis. If people knew, would I lose my job? Would I ever be able to play football again? Would my friends still talk to me? Keeping it all under wraps helped me to be confident in my work. It was an honour to drive in to Croke Park every day and get paid to work for an organisation that had done so much for me, despite the bitterness that grown towards my own playing career.

~

When I was 12 we moved from Dublin to Bailieborough. My parents had grown tired of the capital and wanted a better quality of life for their three boys. My older brother, David, remained behind as he had already left school and was working full time and didn't want to move to the country. Truth was, neither did I, but at that age I had no choice.

On my first day in the town community school I stood outside the red double-doors that guarded the assembly area where the rest of my fellow second-year pupils were gathered. The whole returning year were already divided into their four classes, standing in straight lines and ready for the roll call. I stood rooted to the spot, with a heavy bag packed with all my books for the year, and stared at my new black shoes. I cursed my mother for dropping me off. I felt so out of place.

After the area was cleared and the students had made their way towards their first class of the year, I stood and waited to be told which class I'd be in – like Harry Potter and the students I had read so much about in Hogwarts whose destiny was decided by a Sorting Hat. There were no magical halls, delicious feasts or talking hats for me, though. Instead, there were dozens of Cavan people talking in funny accents, who for some reason unknown to me were all carrying books in their hands rather than in a bag.

After some confusion I was assigned a class and arrived for my first French lesson later than everyone else. Most of the seats were already taken. After a quick scan of the room I slotted in beside a young lad with a baby face who I could see was cursing his luck at having to be the one to put up with the new kid. Silence lingered as we waited for the teacher to appear. It was obvious that one of us had to say something to ease the tension.

'What's your name again?' he said.

'Alan. What's yours?'

'Niall.'

'Nice to meet you,' I replied. I was thrilled his accent wasn't anywhere near as thick as some of the others I had heard that morning, so it was a little easier to strike up a conversation – but not by much. I hadn't a clue what to say to him next, so again I sat there quietly.

'Do you like football?' he asked.

'I do, yeah.'

I was never as grateful to have been asked that question in all of my life. I could see the relief on his face. He looked like he had just dodged a bullet and followed up with a second question.

'You any good?'

'Yeah, not bad. I play a lot of football.'

'Football or soccer?' said Niall.

'What do you mean? Football *is* soccer, like.'

He explained to me how in this part of the country when people said 'football' it always meant Gaelic football, not the stuff Manchester United and Arsenal played. Our two cultures were coming together beautifully!

'I play mostly soccer, but I play Gaelic too,' I replied.

'Sweet. You should join our team. Most of us play both.'

'Yeah, I definitely will.'

And just like that, as the teacher walked into the room, I had my first friend in the place I now called home.

We went on to win the under-14 school title that year, beating Virginia College in the final. Winning helped me form a bond with the lads. I knew it helped that I was talented on the field too, but to this day, Niall O'Reilly, whom I met in that French class, Danny Hanley, Niall Kelly, Sean Cooney, Shane Gray and Barry Tully remain among my circle of friends.

After our success I quickly fell in love with the GAA in Cavan, and I doubt I would have settled into the area as easily without it. It didn't take me long to get signed up for the local GAA club either, Bailieborough Shamrocks, when the season got up and running in the new year.

When I was a kid, the GAA helped me to make friends and gave me a hobby I was extremely passionate about. When we moved from Dublin to Cavan, there were so many benefits to playing the game: the friendships, the fun, the feeling of winning, the respect, the camaraderie. It also brought with it a social standing that I had not experienced before. Later in life I would have struggled to get by financially in college without the scholarship support provided by DIT, Cadbury's and the Gaelic Players Association.

The college had given me modest financial support each year for playing, and I was looked after just as well as many of the more high-profile players because I was so committed to the club off the field. In my four years at DIT, I volunteered as public relations officer and chairman, as well as a selector for the 2010 All-Ireland-winning fresher team. After that I was the manager for two seasons, which ended with a heartbreaking one-point defeat in both a quarter-final and semi-final. For my work in these roles I was nominated by DIT for an additional bursary from Cadbury's, whose scholarship programme covered nine third-level institutions. I was one of 16 students to receive an award of €1,000. The money went some way towards covering my rent for the year – mainly because we had eight lads living in a four-bedroomed house, even though the landlord thought there were only five of us! Cavan men, eh?

While being a GAA player definitely helped me develop socially in my teens and opened up different avenues for financial support when I was a student, it also gave me vital access to the counselling service that the GPA provided free of charge in my time of crisis.

When depression stepped back into the ring for a second bout in early 2012, I'd been caught with my guard down. Thankfully I'd known what to do straight away. There had been no fear or worry. I hadn't spent hours agonising over whether to make the call. There had been no stigma or taboo in my mind. I'd gone back to Niall. I'd gotten back to the room. While I could clearly see how the GAA benefited me at different stages off the field, at the beginning of 2012, my relationship with the game had changed for the worse.

~

When preparations started for the 2012 season my mind was completely occupied with trying to overcome my depression, and I knew I would not be playing football for Cavan. I knew I'd needed a break from the expectations I put on myself when it came to playing. My Sigerson Cup adventure ended in February with a loss to DCU and, ironically, I had played particularly well in that last game. I'd saved a penalty low down to my right from Dublin's Dean Rock to keep us in the contest when we were under serious pressure, and had made another reflex save from his fellow All-Ireland winner Eoghan O'Gara.

As we'd trotted towards the changing room at half-time, the manager, Paul Clancy, marched alongside me and put his arm around my shoulder. 'Good man. You're after keeping us in the game there.'

'No bother. Sure, that's what I'm there for,' I replied calmly.

It had surprised me how I was still capable of pulling good performances out of the bag when they were needed. I mean, there were days when I felt there was no way I could muster the energy to answer the phone or even have a shower, never mind train or play football. At that stage it was clear that depression wasn't ruining my ability, just my passion and enjoyment. For years my body had been trained as a ball-stopping machine, so when I was playing, my muscle memory often made decisions before my brain knew what was happening.

Sometimes I saved a shot and felt absolutely nothing. It was like the heart and soul had been ripped from my body. On other occasions I would get a rare surge of adrenaline that would remind me of how playing in goals used to make me feel like I was the king of the world. Soon after a good save, that injection of mood-enhancing endorphins would be replaced by guilt. I would think about how I now lacked any real conviction about continuing in football and what a waste of talent that was. It got worse when I conceded a goal, as the other voice in my head told me I would have saved it if I cared about football as much as I used to; I was a fraud living off my previous achievements.

It was a vicious circle. I was damned if I did, damned if I didn't.

After the DIT match when we were knocked out of the Sigerson Cup, I'd also quit playing with my club, Bailieborough Shamrocks, as I'd felt I needed to get away from the game and all the mental baggage it brought with it in terms of preparation and performance. I wanted to give the counselling process the time and energy it needed, so I decided to try life without football for a few months. In 12 months

I had gone from giving everything I had to play for my county to not playing at all. I needed a break from it and I wanted to regain a sense of normality. With football during that time, the lows were as low as ever but the highs were bringing little joy. The balance was wrong. I thought that just getting away from the game and being a 'normal' person for a while would help me to feel, well, normal. I used my old injury problems as an excuse to step away, saying I needed time to address them in order for me to come back in top form. I was slowly growing stronger thanks to counselling, but I wanted to avoid the ups and downs that naturally came with the game. Stepping away meant that I didn't have to worry about winning or losing or playing well; life just seemed easier without it.

My depression remained a secret but I told those involved with Cavan and Bailieborough Shamrocks that I was struggling with injuries and felt burned out, which was partly true but far from the whole story. I did confide in Paul Kelly, a selector on the club team. He was the father of one of my best friends, Niall, and he had coached me when I was younger. I asked him to keep it to himself.

'Don't worry about rushing back to football,' he'd said. 'Getting better and over this is far more important, so take your time, Alo. There are more important things than football sometimes.'

I'd thanked him and told him I was just going through a tough period, that I just needed some time to figure it all out.

'Look after yourself, kiddo, and stay in touch,' was all he'd said.

I was so happy with how understanding he'd been. My character and commitment to football were openly questioned by my fellow clubmen, but I have no hard feelings about that. I know now that it's hard to understand somebody else's situation and show empathy towards them if they're not being honest about what is happening, and I had been lying through my teeth in order to avoid playing.

The break definitely did me good, but as I watched both Bailieborough and Cavan throughout the season, the itch to get back playing gradually returned.

~

Midway through the 2012 season Val was shown the door. Even though I wasn't part of the panel, I knew that some of the players had started to find the setup and mood of the team really bewildering. Val had genuine passion for Cavan football, and had decided controversially to cut players at the start of the 2012 season, a decision that had upset a lot of people. I will always respect him for making that courageous choice after we barely avoided relegation to the basement division and were subsequently hammered twice in the championship, to Donegal in Ulster and Longford in the qualifiers, during his first year in charge. Tactically we were extremely naïve at senior level, and the game plan didn't seem to be evolving – it all just felt a bit ad hoc. At the other end of the spectrum entirely was the Donegal senior team now under the tutelage of Jim McGuinness; they cruised past us with nine points to spare thanks to the system he had implemented against us at under-21 level in 2010 and 2011.

We had been hovering around the bottom of Division Three before Val arrived, but after 12 months in the job I didn't believe he was going to take Cavan forward in the long term, and I think others had twigged that too. I felt the under-21 management team I had played under was miles ahead of the backroom team that Val had pieced together when taking the job in 2011, and the collective drive and sense of togetherness that arrived with the under-21 players failed to carry across to the senior camp. To be fair; some of the blame goes to the older players and we, as under-21s, would have to absorb some of it as well.

Unfortunately, the difference between us and, say, Tyrone's golden generation was that our young players were going into an unsettled team with a high turnover of managers and players, whereas Tyrone had real leaders like Brian Dooher and Peter Canavan to call upon, and a manager of the calibre of Mickey Harte to guide new panel members. That's what helped them win two All-Ireland under-21 titles and two minor titles between 2000 and 2004 and then the Sam Maguire three times that same decade.

Cavan had huge talent pouring in from the under-21 ranks as well as from the Ulster minor-winning team of 2011, of which my little brother Billy was a part, also as goalkeeper. The most important thing though was that the younger players were coming in with a winning mentality and were determined to change Cavan football for the better – we had all experienced success, and winning breeds confidence in a way few managers can achieve through a team talk.

When Val's exit was confirmed, there really was only one man for the job: Terry had backed up the county's first Ulster title in 14 years by successfully defending the Ulster under-21 crown. With Terry at the helm and in sole charge of the senior team, a call arrived in the summer of 2012 to see if I would be interested in rejoining the panel. The Cavan junior team, which plays in the Leinster junior championship, trained with the senior group and Terry wanted to know if I would get back involved. It was clear that the junior outfit was going to act as a feeder team to the senior side and be utilised to build the emerging talent. I found it hard to say no to him due to our history together, and while I had enjoyed the break from football, deep down, a part of me enjoyed feeling wanted again.

However, just when I was hoping that football would help me feel good about myself again, it kicked me when I was down. I turned up to two games and found myself as deputy to the sub-keeper from that year's under-21 team. Looking back now, my vision was clouded by how desperate I was to experience the joy of wearing the number one jersey again. It was clear my relationship with the game still wasn't what it needed to be for that to happen.

When Cavan reached the All-Ireland junior semi-final against Kerry in August my mood had deteriorated sharply and I made up my mind that I was not travelling with the team to the game. While I loved my new job, adjusting from the college lifestyle to full-time employment during the summer of 2012 brought with it its own set of pressures and complications. My depression had spiked again and I couldn't face the long journey and the thoughts of being an actor for that long. Rather than helping my depression at that stage, football was unsettling the emotional jar that Niall and I had discussed during counselling. I knew I had come back to the game too soon. If I was so unstable while being a substitute, what would I have been like if I was actually going to battle for my county again?

I sent Terry a vague text the day before the match against Kerry, confirming that I wouldn't be there – he knew nothing of my depression. As I sent the text I knew I was letting him and Cavan down, but my battle with depression had to come first. I needed to figure out why returning to the game seemed to fan the flames of my depression. 'Fuck football,' I said to myself as I lay on my bed looking at a poster of my under-21 team celebrating our Ulster victory on the field.

The waves of depression continued. I had some good days and some bad days, but I was yet to achieve a prolonged spell of 'normality' or 'good form'. It was all very topsy-turvy.

In a club game later that month against Crosserlough in the Cavan intermediate championship, our keeper went down with a groin injury in the second half and yours truly was summoned from the bench. When the call came I was eating a Nutri-Grain bar that I had discovered in my pocket and was talking rubbish to two other subs – not even watching the game. I had no jersey on and was wearing a pair of old boots I had since I was a minor in 2007. I soon realised I shouldn't have been on the pitch. I wasn't ready and I didn't deserve it. I thought back to all the work I had done to return from surgery for the Cavan under-21s, the graft I had put in to make such an impression on my first game back. I realised I was a bigger joke than the Cavan footballers who had ordered all that pizza in Limerick. For the final 20 minutes I was like a rabbit in the headlights. A year earlier I had been in the best shape of my life, playing in an All-Ireland final, and now I was a sub for my club team for a lad who usually played outfield – and a bad sub at that. By late September I had moved away from the constant hopelessness that had consumed me, but even though I was still far from where I wanted to be, I was constantly weighing up the pros and cons of returning to the Cavan set-up for the 2013 season.

During the summer, Donegal had again knocked Cavan out of Ulster – this time by six points. Terry and his management team had taken over from Val too late in the year to truly put a stamp on things. Our qualifier win over neighbours Fermanagh, in which a number of the younger players excelled, was a big morale-boost and gave a glimmer of hope as the likes of Gearoid McKiernan, Jack Brady, Eugene Keating and Niall McDermott all showed well. In all, nine of the players involved in our under-21 campaign in 2011 played in that win. Thirteen of the 19 players that featured had graduated from the under-21 classes of 2010, 2011 and 2012, all of which had been managed by Terry. Despite being hammered by 17 points at home to Kildare, I could see a new Cavan team was emerging. Although I'd been absent for much of the year, I was proud of them for making the step up on that day and for being the change that was needed.

Despite my poor performance and commitment with the junior and club team, Terry did call again in October 2012. When I saw his name flash up on my phone I stepped out of the office in Croke Park, went through one of the premium boxes on Level 6 of the stadium and sat out on the leather seats on the balcony overlooking the pitch.

He wanted me on the senior team for pre-season training ahead of the 2013 campaign.

I knew he believed that, in the past, I had brought good character and leadership to a dressing room. I was always hopeful the phone would ring, because, in my heart, I hoped I had earned another chance as a result of my service record under him with the under-21 team. I kept assuring myself that he had to remember the Fermanagh and Wexford games during the 2011 under-21 campaign when I dug us out of trouble.

My reply to Terry was immediate. I told him I wanted the opportunity to play for him again as I firmly believed we could transform the senior camp from that which I experienced under Tommy Carr and then Val Andrews. I wanted to be a part of that process.

However, rather than sounding happy at my acceptance of the offer, Terry paused for a second. 'No, Alan, I mean are you really interested?' he asked calmly.

Silence.

I knew what he was getting at. He was talking about my lack of commitment to the junior team earlier in the year, and obviously to the fact that I had barely played any football in 2012.

As we chatted, I was sitting almost directly behind the goals where I had made that unbelievable save in the All-Ireland final when I deflected the ball onto the crossbar. It was a powerful and positive memory, and I was certain that I wanted to feel that rush again, but how could I explain all that to Terry?

Should I let him think I just got carried away with myself after our Ulster win and spent a year thinking I was a big-time Charlie who just went on the lash? Do I mention the injury struggles and how they stopped me enjoying football? Or do I just tell him the truth?

I decided on the truth.

Was this a conversation I could even have with an inter-county manager? Could I tell him I was living with depression and still battling the demons – and that I would be for the foreseeable future? Was it okay to admit to him that I had been in counselling for large parts of 2012? Would he think I was less of a man because of it? Would he withdraw his offer for me to rejoin the panel? Did I come with more baggage than I was worth?

I took a deep breath and blew it out slowly down the phone. As I looked out at the most glorious, beautiful field in the world, I let Terry Hyland, sole Cavan senior manager, know what I felt was still my dirty, big, shameful secret.

There was no deep, meaningful conversation with him or anything like that, but he was understanding and compassionate. I remember the end of the call vividly. 'We'll see you Friday, then, and we'll go at it from there,' he ordered.

At first the relief was huge. I could physically feel the tension leave my chest as I breathed out. So much stigma and fear had built up in my mind about this moment, so often had I considered all the terrible knock-on effects of being honest about my situation, about my vulnerabilities. I thought about the shame and guilt of being an inter-county footballer not fit to handle the demands of the modern game.

But before I could enjoy the sense of release, the moment was interrupted by that voice again. *Don't bother. Football isn't worth the hassle. You don't deserve to be a senior inter-county player.*

I was furious. If that voice belonged to someone standing in front of me, I would have punched him straight in the face. It was time to take a stand against the belittling remarks and insidious thoughts. I was sick and tired of that voice and the things it said holding me back, of the negativity it tried to inject into my life. I wanted to unshackle myself from the chains and get back to doing what I had always done best. Terry was giving me a perfect opportunity to do just that, and I wanted to take it. I took a deep breath and returned my focus to the phone conversation. Terry had no idea of the entirely different conversation that was raging in my mind.

The good voice took over. 'You will, Terry. You will. See you Friday,' I replied emphatically.

And just like that, I was a member of the Cavan senior football team again. I had taken another step in the right direction. I was proud of all I had achieved since that December day in 2011 when I could have ended it all. I felt better after adding one more person to my circle of trust.

Then what I had just signed up for hit me. A twice-nominated All-Star in the shape of Drung clubman and Railway Cup goalkeeper James Reilly was in the way of me getting my hands on that number one Cavan jersey again.

Challenge accepted.

8
The Comeback Kid

Christmas 2012 had been a particularly difficult period for my depression and despite all the progress I felt I had made over the course of the year through counselling and rejoining the Cavan panel, things began to unravel during the festive season. I had struggled to feel the same elation that others felt and old demons reared their heads again. I had left the pub where so many others were happy, had wandered aimlessly into the darkness of the night and had come close to ending my life for a second time.

Just a week on from that miserable walk home from the pub in Bailieborough and that suicidal urge, I stood wearing my number one jersey in front of a couple of hundred people and pretended I was absolutely fine. I felt like a con artist. A few nights previously, my suicidal thoughts had become suicidal feelings and those feelings had then manifested into an urge. Thankfully, however, I had somehow managed to stop that from transforming into action.

On Sunday, 6 January 2013 I made my Cavan senior debut against Down in the opening round of the McKenna Cup.

I had worked incredibly hard in the previous months to get myself into decent shape despite all the obstacles I had to overcome in my head. When I had walked away from football at the start of 2012 I had also taken my foot off the gas in terms of personal fitness and the maintenance work needed to keep my groin troubles in check. Going back to the Cavan panel meant a significant lifestyle change as well as finding the motivation to go to the group gym sessions after work on Mondays, and training on Wednesdays and Fridays. With the increased training load, I needed to do my own light work in the gym and pool on Tuesdays and Thursdays to ensure a proper recovery and to reduce the risk of my injury returning.

There were so many occasions, particularly in the first few weeks after returning to the panel, when I still thought about walking away from it all. I hadn't answered the questions about what a football career was worth to me, whether or not it took up too much of my time. I still wondered what else I had to offer the world.

The negative voice was always there, of course, and it told me I didn't enjoy the game anymore and fed me reasons to quit and ways to do it. All I had to do was say I was injured again, or tell Terry it was all too much for me, but something deep within me kept urging me to go on. After countless hours in the therapy room, my gut feeling was growing stronger against all the negative thoughts. In the end, I trusted it.

When I got home after a day at work, it sometimes took a colossal effort to force myself to change into my football gear and make the trip to Parnell's GAA club, which was, at the time, our training base in Dublin. The gym and the football pitch seemed like the last places on earth I should be going given that I was so short of energy. If I was tired, should I not stay at home and let my body rest and recover? I would sit on the end of the bed for a few minutes, looking at my training gear and weighing up whether I should stay or go.

Depression doesn't always exist in the realm of logic, so even though it was counter-intuitive, I never felt any worse when I had completed the training session. I certainly am not saying football made me feel better every time, because it didn't, but it wasn't actively lowering my mood any more – and that was progress.

Committing to the Cavan cause was also beneficial in another aspect of life: it helped me avoid the internal conversations that often came when I sat idle.

I could recognise many of the positive things football brought to my life, how it enhanced my weekly routine and gave me an increased sense of direction, focus and structure. The sense of routine was really helpful. Of course there was the odd night when I went through the motions at sessions, but more often than not it felt as if I had slotted myself into autopilot – in a good way. Depression had made me aimless, and I'd spent so much of my year since that DIT training camp drifting, that it was good to be reminded about what it took to train as an inter-county player and to work within a group that was looking to excel. It was like I was back where I belonged, and I felt proud that I had not let depression prevent me from fulfilling this opportunity. In the early stages of the season, we trained every Monday and Wednesday in Dublin, and then on Friday and Sunday in Cavan, so I only had to distract myself on Tuesdays and Thursdays, because I was spending my weekends at home with my family. I was delighted to be back shoulder to shoulder with the likes of Niall Murray, Niall McDermott and Gearoid McKiernan, whom I had an awful lot of time for as footballers and men. It just felt right for us to be rowing the boat in the same direction for Cavan football. Besides, allowing myself to get caught up in preparations for an upcoming game made it easier to forget about what had gone on in my own personal life. On the whole, it was a busy schedule that kept me occupied and in good company, but doubts began to creep back in towards the end of that year.

Having endured the winter slog, which is by far the least glamorous or enjoyable time for an inter-county player, I was extremely nervous when it came to playing Down in the first game of 2013. I was more nervous than before any other game. Ever. Standing in the middle of a freezing Kingspan Breffni Park stadium, on a pitch that hadn't wintered well, I was not in a good place mentally for my competitive debut.

When I put on that jersey I'm being entrusted by my team and our supporters to be calm, confident and alert for the players I stand behind. That is my duty, and it used to be a responsibility I thrived on, along with the excitement of the game. Saving shots and tipping balls away from danger is obviously a huge part of being a quality number one on the team, but I also loved the anticipation aspect of goalkeeping: trying to read plays, spot runs and instantaneously communicate all of it to the defence so that we could stop scores together before they had a chance to materialise.

However, as much as I tried to get the blood up for my debut, I just couldn't focus. I listened to the pre-game team talk, which was all about 'laying down a marker' and 'starting the year off well' but the game was no longer life or death for me. I had played my own game of that just a week before.

One half of me was certainly thrilled to be back between the sticks, but the other part, fuelled by that little voice in my head, was freaking out. At times during the game I was a self-doubting, self-loathing bag of nerves. When I had started in two Ulster minor and two under-21 championship campaigns I had felt I was the natural choice for the Cavan number one jersey, but that confidence had gone and I no longer thought I was the person who would take the jersey from James Reilly and go on to have a long and successful career.

I don't think I wanted the ball to come near me. Or maybe I did. Would a nice early touch settle me down? I tried to recall the Meath game when I had made my comeback in 2011 for the under-21s and reassured myself that it was all going to be okay. I tried to remember the sense of confidence and belief I'd had back then. I thought of all the training I had done in the previous three months to be trusted to wear the jersey again. All those hours in the gym and the number of times I'd dived into the muck after a ball, desperate to rediscover the joy that playing this sport had once brought me. I reminded myself that I deserved it, that I was where I was meant to be.

My head was spinning. Did our supporters think I was worthy of wearing this jersey? I worried that some of them might also have been there for that game against Crosserlough with my club. God, that day was embarrassing; I had fallen so far. Do any of these supporters even rate me? Do I even rate myself?

Relax, Alan, you have this. Take a deep breath and trust yourself. It's normal to be nervous after a long break out of the game. It is going to take some time to find your rhythm.

I tried to concentrate on more upbeat memories from my playing past – hoping that the positive reinforcement would stop whatever it was that had taken over me. The memories were all well and good, but I was alarmed at how the game no longer felt natural to me. This simply did not feel right. It was all completely alien.

Relax, Alan. Relax. Just breathe. You're going to be fine. You have this. Whatever this is, it will pass. Deep breaths, lad. Just focus on the next ball and start talking to the lads.

I managed to focus on the game and watched Down move possession towards my goal. As they edged closer to our 45-metre line, a forward made a burst towards space and Oisin Minagh had yet to see him as he was playing the man from in front. 'Right, Minagh. Right!'

Oisin reacted immediately and cut off a diagonal ball. He had started as corner-back for my very first Ulster minor championship game back in 2007 against the same opposition, and was at full-back for the entire under-21 campaign in 2011; we had built up a lot of trust over the years. He too had been drifting in and out of the Cavan senior team since our Ulster victory due to injuries, so 2013 was very much a comeback year for him as well. I wondered if he was as anxious as me about his return to action. It was hard to imagine, though, because he looked so comfortable tussling with his man. Doubts and more doubts came at me.

Early in the first half I had to take a kick-out. This is one of the strongest parts of my game; years of practice had built up my accurate and reliable strike. I knew that I needed to remind the management of that if I was to become a permanent fixture on the team. It was one of the major advantages I had over the far more experienced James Reilly, who was a colossal man with a more traditional kick-out that travelled farther, but had less accuracy than mine.

As I went to execute it, my standing foot slipped in the mud where the grass should have been on the 14-metre line. As soon as the ball took flight, I was on my way down. Aiming for the right side of midfield, I hooked the ball and it landed in the central area – straight into the arms of a red-and-black jersey. The kick travelled the guts of 50 metres. There were still eight Cavan men between the ball and my net, but Down somehow ran it straight back through us and then sliced us open with a killer pass. The move finished when Paul McComiskey hammered it into the top corner and the umpire to my right raised the green flag. I had recovered from my slip to take up a good position in between the posts for the shot, but I was buried. It was a rude awakening, how ruthless the game could be at this level – mistakes were punished. I bent over to pick the ball out of the goals.

You don't belong here anymore. That goal was your fault.

I agreed, and told myself it was a terrible kick, but I knew I needed to get that negative voice out of my head for the next play. I had to restart the game and I couldn't let the voice hijack the rest of my performance. It meant too much and I had worked too hard. I blocked it all out and got a decent strike on the ball – it sailed out to the stand side of the pitch and we secured possession thanks to an excellent leap from Gearoid McKiernan who was leading our midfield. 'That's the boy, G,' I roared as soon as he off-loaded possession.

He turned back to me and gave the thumbs up. Nobody had caught more of my kick-outs than him as we had played for Cavan minors, under-21s, DIT freshers and the DIT Sigerson teams together. With all that practice, we had a great understanding on the field. That simple gesture settled me down and my anxiety gradually eased as the game wore on.

As soon as the final whistle sounded though, and a two-point loss was confirmed, I heard that voice again as I picked my tees and water bottle out of the goal and headed for the sanctuary of the changing rooms. *You cost us the game, Alan.*

It was a poor kick, absolutely, but there had been so many things that needed to happen for them to score – so many variables that could have gone our way, but didn't. It was sheer and utter bad luck, and nobody gave the slightest indication that they felt the goal was my fault, except the voice in my head. It was all I heard for hours after the defeat. As I changed out of my gear under the main stand, showered, ate my post-match meal in silence surrounded by the rest of the team and then headed home in the car, the voice was all I heard. I was devastated, and my mood began to plummet.

As I stopped off for petrol in Cavan town after the game, I bumped into Kevin Meehan, a fellow member of the class of 2011, who had also started that day.

'What did you make of that?' he asked.

'Same shit, different year,' I said pessimistically and rolled my eyes up at the sky, disillusioned with football and how the Cavan senior team had again failed to emerge victorious.

He too was disappointed with the result, but he wasn't as down about it as I was. He told me to keep my head up and keep working at it. On the drive home I blamed the result for making me feel as low as I did. I thought about all the counselling that I had gone through and wondered where all my positivity had gone. Why did I doubt myself so much?

For as long as I can remember, I have been my harshest critic. I remember sitting in the back of the car as a nine-year-old, huffing after I had lost a soccer game. My parents, sitting in the two front seats, had tried to get me talking but I had ignored them completely and kept flicking the button that controlled the window beside me.

'Don't be upset because you lost the game. You played well; it was the fault of the players out the field. Sure, what can you do if there are two of them and only one of you?' said Mam.

I snapped at her and was duly told off by my father. They left me to concentrate on my sulk after that.

I had often felt that I should have stopped a goal that nobody expected me to, but I always tried to learn from those and move on – switching my focus to the next match.

Between Kingspan Breffni Park and my house in Cavan I pulled over to send Kevin a direct message on Twitter. I told him to pull me up on that sort of negative talk if he heard it from me again. He was a good person to mention this to, as we always sat near each other in one corner of the main dressing room.

I was beginning to get used to living with my depression on a daily basis, and I was learning all the time how to better manage and cope with it. I knew I had to figure out how to shut that voice out during matches.

Just a week after I had avoided the magnetic pull of the oncoming car, I was more adamant than ever that depression wasn't going to take my life or stop me from playing for Cavan, either.

9

The Rollercoaster

Playing for Cavan was an honour and privilege that ignited a unique passion within me. Playing let me become the physical embodiment of my county and encapsulate the spirit of my tribe. I wanted to stick my chest out and show everyone how ready for battle we were, and how committed to one another.

I do it for identity: to pull on the jersey and wear the crest and colours with pride. We go to war together. We break our bones, pull muscles and sprain ligaments. We live some dreams and have others crushed. We all know there will be tears of joy along with tears of sorrow, that it's a rollercoaster full of highs and lows. Yet despite all the doubts and fears that were amplified by my depression, I had successfully buckled up for the ride of the 2013 season with the Cavan senior football team.

By the time the National League came around in the first week of February, Cavan's long-standing keeper, James Reilly, had played in our only other

McKenna Cup game against Armagh as Queen's University had failed to field against us. Despite having won this second game, we failed to advance from the group as a result of our defeat to Down.

When the team was announced for the opening league game, the management elected to go with the more experienced pair of hands in goals and throughout most of the team. Just four players who had put Ulster underage medals into their pockets in the previous two years started the game.

In my mind there was no doubt that I had worked harder than James for the jersey over the previous number of months. I would have been a bit of a gamble, but I was deeply hurt by the rejection when I had invested so much in my return to the squad. That said, my less-than-brilliant performance against Down probably made Terry's decision easier.

It got worse for me when we went out to train immediately after the line-up was announced on the Friday evening. During that session a practice game was set up with two goals no more than 30 metres apart, but most of the shots went in at one end as all the attackers had been put on the same team. I was standing in between those cones, and my team – the defensive team – would only become attackers to the far goal if they successfully intercepted a ball or turned over possession. If they didn't, then the other keeper would sit idle watching the madness unfold of what was basically three-on-three in a confined space.

Shots rained in relentlessly, and eventually I took one full force to the face. I couldn't see as my eyes blurred with tears, like only a smack from a size-5 O'Neills ball to the nose can do. The drill continued and I kept going, squinting to see the ball and make some saves, but I was scrambling around like a headless chicken. Eventually I had to sit down and wave the white flag. I needed a minute to regain control of my sight and make sure I was okay. As my eyes cleared I saw James standing with his arms crossed in the goals at the opposite end, chatting away to one of the other lads while Alan Clarke, a defender, had filled in as a keeper while I was down. It was just dumb luck that I had ended up in the busy goal, but it also served to rub extra salt into the wound.

At inter-county level the goalkeepers spend a huge amount of time together, as we train separately from the rest of the team for the majority of sessions and rejoin the group when needed for drills, conditioned games or to practise kick-out routines.

James and myself were wired differently when it came to training, but we always got on really well and shared a room when we were on away trips. However, at that moment I wanted to rip his head off his shoulders. He had no idea how I was feeling, but I was just so desperate to be given the jersey that I felt he had taken from me. I was furious, and as soon as training was over I packed up my bag and headed out the door.

'How the fuck am I not playing ahead of him?' I shouted as I slammed my hand off the steering wheel in frustration as I drove up the hill at the back of the stadium.

I drove home aggressively, faster than I should have. Halfway home I slipped off the main road so I could tear into a narrow country lane even harder. I knew it rarely had any traffic on it and even if it did, I would see the headlights coming miles away in the dark night. This road rage was all because I hadn't been picked to play a game. I failed to realise how abnormal my relationship with football still was as I burned rubber like somebody possessed.

Paranoia kicked in. Was Terry not picking me because I had depression? Did he not trust me anymore? Was I a liability to the team? Should I just quit now and be done with it because the comeback experiment had failed? I should never have rejoined the panel. It just wasn't me anymore.

I didn't realise it, but it clearly wasn't healthy how much I needed that starting spot to help me feel good about myself. So much of my confidence, ego, morale, worth and identity was completely interlinked with that jersey. My recovery over the previous months had taught me so much, but clearly not enough. Despite everything I had learned, I was back to needing football to go well in order for me to be even remotely happy with my life.

I stormed into the house and slammed my bag

onto the floor as Mam and Dad sat peacefully on the couch.

'What's wrong with you?' Dad asked.

'Nothing.'

'Then why are you stomping around and banging doors?'

'I'm not.'

'You are.'

'He hasn't fucking picked me. I'm not on the team.'

'Did he say anything to you?'

'Nope. Not a word.' My eyes filled up with tears. 'I'm going to quit. I don't need this shit.'

'Relax. It's only the first game. You'll get a chance,' my father assured me.

I could count on my fingers the number of times I had been a backup goalkeeper in a game of any importance.

Despite my disappointment, despite my rage, I remembered the lesson I had learned the previous year with my club when I had come on as a replacement. I hadn't prepared myself properly. I took a deep breath, determined that I would capitalise on any opportunity that came my way, take the knock to my pride this time and come out ready the next time.

What Dad had said proved to be prophetic as James went down injured 49 minutes into the match against Antrim. I came on and made my league debut for Cavan in an utterly forgettable game that we lost by two points.

Despite the floundering start, the training and attitude was the best it had ever been in the senior setups since I had become involved, and a huge part of that was the new management team who had set about changing attitudes and expectations.

Everybody knew we had to bounce back with a big performance if we were going to be taken seriously. Thankfully, after our bitter disappointment against Antrim, two big fixtures were coming up and I was in goals for both games, as James's injury had ruled him out. I knew I had to put in a good performance as the injury was only minor and I knew he would recover in a short space of time.

Our neighbours Monaghan were next up. We comfortably dispatched them, 1-10 to 0-5, in front of a lively crowd in Kingspan Breffni Park under the Saturday-night lights. When the final whistle sounded there was serious delight in our team. As I soaked it all up after the game, I couldn't help but feel how far this dressing room had evolved since 2011. The underage success in the county had re-energised the players across the board, and the honesty and work rate that had been the backbone of securing the under-21 titles had become a strong attribute of the senior team.

As I headed home afterwards I was buzzing. It was the first time in nearly two years that I had got lost in the moment of a game. Of course I still had doubts, but I felt like I was getting closer to what I call 'my zone' and reinstalling the best version of me in goals. It was in complete contrast to the last time I had run out in the same stadium, just a week after I had almost ended my life.

Even more pleasing was the fact that we showed a sense of togetherness and intensity that night that I don't think Cavan supporters had seen from their senior team for many years. I was delighted to get my full debut and leave the pitch with a clean sheet. My self-confidence and belief were starting to return and I wondered if that McKenna Cup experience against Down was just a once-off.

But then next up was Meath, another bitter rival, seven days later and we had a real pep in our step after the Monaghan win. The hard work the team had put in before Christmas with trainer Peter Donnelly, an All-Ireland winner with Tyrone and a top-class coach, was really showing and there was no denying we were fitter than the other teams at that stage of the season.

This time, around ten of the 20 who featured over the 70 minutes were from the under-21 classes of 2011 and 2012. Another four were from the Cavan under-21 team that had lost to the Jim McGuinness-inspired Donegal team in the 2010 Ulster under-21 final. Youth was definitely getting its chance and Terry and his team of Joe McCarthy, Anthony Forde and Padraig Dolan had carried across the sense of honesty and empowerment that they prided themselves on. Of our 15 scores, nine came from players who had ended the county's trophy famine in 2011. We were the change, just as we had talked about so often growing up.

While results on the pitch were taking a swift turn for the better, the situation in my head continued to fluctuate. On the bus to Navan for the Meath game, anxiety had started to creep in again. I'd had a slight niggle in my groin as I'd tweaked the muscle during the Monaghan game, but it was the type of injury I had played through successfully so many times over the years. In fact, I had played through injuries much more severe than that without a second's hesitation – all the way back to when I was 11 and took the protective brace off my fractured thumb so I could play matches, before putting it back on for the rest of the week, or until the next game. Was the depression and anxiety making the injury feel worse than it was?

We got off to an unbelievable start and by half-time we were 0-10 to 0-1 to the good. As we took the battle to Meath and showed them what the new Cavan was all about, they grew frustrated. When they tapped over their only point of the half from a free, one of their players tried to rally the troops. 'Fuck's sake, come on! This is only Cavan, boys. Cavan!' he said.

At that moment I wanted nothing more than to go home with the two points on the board so we could stick it to that condescending fool.

Meath did breach our goals in the second half, and I kept wondering to myself if I should have stopped it, if it was my fault. As a keeper I couldn't dwell on previous plays; I simply had to live in the moment and let my anticipation levels keep me a fraction of a second ahead of the others.

Goalkeepers have to make pressurised decisions all the time; they just can't second-guess themselves, as their trusting relationship with the defence would deteriorate, and the opposition supporters and attackers would start to feed off the confusion.

I was annoyed that my first year playing senior football with Cavan should be marred by doubt when I should have been coming into my own. It wasn't meant to be this way. Years ago I would have been in my element in these pressurised situations. I had such a calm aura about me back then, but it seemed that my depression had altered that.

I remembered back to the time the minor selector for Cavan Paul McCorry had spoken to me in the moments before throw in for our championship opener against Antrim in 2008. 'Best of luck today,' he'd said.

I'd shaken his hand, cracked a smile and winked as I fixed the peaked cap on my head to block out the sun that was beaming down in Casement Park. He'd stopped on the spot and looked at me. 'You love this, don't you?'

I'd smiled again.

'Forget about luck, you belong out here. This

is where you are meant to be. Enjoy it,' and he'd walked off towards the sideline.

And enjoy it I did.

Worrying if the management held me responsible for the Meath goal, I was determined to make my presence felt on the next ball that dropped in. Right on cue, one dropped short to the edge of the square and was heading straight into the outstretched hands of Joe Sheridan. I raced out, accelerating off my line as fast as I could. 'Keeper's!' I roared as I jumped and put my knee into his back like all good keepers are coached to do. The ball was comfortably punched to the safety of the left wing.

That one decision and action put me at ease and did so much for my conviction. My anxiety dissolved almost immediately and I could focus on keeping Meath at bay.

And we outworked and outclassed Meath by 0-15 to 1-6.

The panel had been constantly chopping and changing over the years but we'd never found the right balance. Monaghan and Meath were two big scalps for us – especially for a number of players who, like me, had still not started many games at this level and were gaining vital experience. Not only that, but older players like Alan Clarke, Ronan Flanagan, Cian Mackey, Martin Reilly, Mark McKeever and Thomas Corr were really stepping up to become serious leaders for the emerging talent both on and off the pitch. It was almost as if everyone was stepping into a new role, and despite so many of the faces being the same, somehow it all felt fresh.

It was brilliant to see it all coming together. I think the management had finally pieced together the right blend of youth and experience. It felt like the dawn of a new era, and I was so happy to be a part of it. I didn't feel like an under-21 player on the senior panel anymore. I was part of a team again.

After the game, I couldn't believe how close I had come to declaring myself unfit in the build-up. Was I ever going to see the end of the two voices in my mind? Was I ever going to trust my own instincts again? Whatever about learning to live with it and manage what was going on in my head in my normal life, I didn't like having it with me on the field one bit.

On 9 March, the day before I was due to make my third straight league start for Cavan, my relationship with my girlfriend ended for good, about a year after we had got back together. Just when things were starting to come right on the field for me, the game of life began to unravel. I will always appreciate what we had together over the years. It can't have been easy for a 20-year-old to deal with the baggage I brought to the relationship in that final year we had together. For long periods I was not the happy, cheeky and carefree kid she had fallen in love with.

There was no huge argument – I rarely remember arguing with her about anything – but after much confusion and lots of conversation we both reached a stage where we could see that we wanted different things in life. We had spent most of our formative years together and she wanted some time to discover who she was as an individual, away from the comfort and security that our relationship brought. It made sense and I fully understood where she was coming from.

I respected her for having the courage to make that decision, for knowing what was best for her. The split was something I thought could be good for me too, at least in the abstract, but I was also terrified about what life would be like without her. It was a huge step into the unknown, and I wasn't sure if I was ready or able for that. Not having her to fall back on was a scary proposition, as was the absence of real, meaningful conversations.

I told myself I would worry about processing how I felt after I had got through the upcoming match with Sligo with another clean sheet.

We were desperate for another two points as we were now in the promotion hunt. However, we failed to rediscover our form from the previous two games and we were down 1-5 to 0-6 at the interval. After the restart I made one of my best saves as my reflexes took over and I reached full length, diving to my left and managing to claw away what would have been a certain goal. It felt amazing. The adrenaline raced through my veins as I got a pat on the head from James McEnroe for getting us out of jail with a save I had no right to make.

'That's the boy,' he said.

I roared at other defenders, telling them we had to

lift our game. I wasn't thinking of the past or the future. I was there in that exact moment – precisely where I had to be, where I wanted to be. It was the euphoric feeling that football used to give me, another brief reminder of how I felt during that under-21 season. It felt so good to feel that way again. It was electrifying. I was back in the swing of things. After all the dark days, I was settling into the role that I always wanted – to be Cavan's number one. I was doing it. I was living my dream.

A few minutes later a high ball came in from the right side of the pitch under the main stand in Markievicz Park. I rose as high as I could for what should have been a routine catch, but as I jumped, my line of sight moved above the shade that the covered stand provided, and the glaring sun slipped under my blue Cavan hat and beamed straight into my eyes. I could see nothing for what felt like an eternity. All I could go on was my sense of touch and sound.

The ball rebounded off my chest and the Sligo forward clattered me. I fell back, seeing nothing, and put my hand out to both soften the impact and help me get back on my feet as quickly as I could in case the ball was still in play. But as I fell, the sound of the crowd and the Sligo voices on the field confirmed that the ball was looping high over me and into the net to make it 2-7 to 0-8 to the men in black. Next thing I knew, I was lying in a heap in the middle of the goalmouth holding my arm. A supporter behind me, clearly angry at the loss of a goal, shouted at me, 'Ah, get up, will you? There's nothing wrong with you, for fuck's sake.'

I didn't dignify the abuse with a response. Instead I snarled in his direction. The referee stood over me and the team doctor, Philip Carolan, joined us. 'What's up?' he asked.

'Ah, I'm after doing something to my arm. I'll be grand, just give me a minute.'

The adrenaline was pumping through my body. The referee was in good form and told me to take my time as he sipped the bottle of water that Philip had brought with him in his medical bag. I was fuming and in no mood for small talk. I always prided myself on how few errors I made when playing, especially for my county.

My arm started to hurt but instead of thinking about it, I realised we were now chasing the game and needed to get going quickly. I went to get to my feet but ended up on my hunkers again. Something wasn't right. The doctor put his hand on my shoulder. 'Let me see that arm there.'

'Don't bother,' I said, 'I'll be grand.'

I was wearing the green Cavan short-sleeved jersey, plus a black base layer underneath that extended down to my wrist and slipped neatly into my glove. He ignored me and opened the strap on my glove. As he rolled up the black sleeve, I winced. He signalled to the bench that I had to come off.

'I'm not going off, Doc. I'll be grand.'

'What are we doing here, lads?' asked the ref,

whose patience was dwindling now that he had got his sup of water.

My head was buzzing. Could I play through this or not? I wanted to play, but had to decide what was best for the team.

Unfortunately, it was not the first time this had happened. Playing a school game many years earlier, I had broken my arm and had tried to play on. The next time I had caught the ball, the pain had been unbearable and I'd had to ask to leave the field. I had no such luxuries on this day though, as the doctor didn't hesitate to make the call.

'Substitute on the Cavan team. Number 16 James Reilly replaces number one Alan O'Mara,' said the voice over the tannoy.

Those words cut through me. Hot on the heels of a great save, all of a sudden I was rendered useless. In the 56th minute I trudged miserably to the sideline, knowing I had just cost us a goal. I sat on the bench beside the goalkeeping coach Gary Rogers with my arm in a sling. As the adrenaline in my body wore off, the pain began to take over.

My eyes started to well up with tears as my arm wavered between numbness and an overwhelming throbbing pain. Some of the tears were for the pain, I have no doubt about that, but most were born of frustration and disappointment. I sat there thinking of everything that I had gone through – the depression, the hours of counselling, the training and the gym work – to get back in this jersey, only for it to be ended so cruelly, and with a new injury to boot.

I slumped there, a completely forlorn figure, my head against the back of the dugout and my left arm extended over my eyes to hide the hurt on my face. 'You can't be fucking serious,' I mumbled, before driving my foot into the metal railing in front of me.

'Chin up,' said Gary. 'Hopefully it's just a bad sprain.'

'Yeah, hopefully.'

The spiral of negativity hit me hard and fast while the team rallied to claim a draw thanks to a Eugene Keating goal in the dying moments of the game.

The journey home was long and painful as I felt every twist and bump in the road between Sligo town and Cavan General Hospital.

Terry phoned to see how I was doing, and then I sat in the waiting room and tried to stay calm and positive. I crossed my fingers that it wasn't a break but my hopes didn't last long. It was swiftly confirmed that there were multiple fractures in my right wrist and arm, and that I would need to go to Drogheda Hospital as soon as possible, as it was the designated fracture clinic for our region. I spent most of the following days in bed with the curtains pulled, cursing the hard, white shell around my arm. From the peak high of that save, I had come crashing down hard.

Injuries are an inevitable part of sport, but rather than simply stopping me from playing the game, I felt that my broken arm was going to prevent me from being the real me – that it would stop me from being content, from experiencing all the positive things that football brought into my life. Because so much of my weekly focus and energy was channelled directly into one area, my freak fall had taken a lot from me.

I had willingly signed up for the rollercoaster when Terry phoned me, but I had not considered the possibility that it could derail so quickly. It was time to buckle up once more.

10
The Truth

For days I lay in the darkness of my bedroom cursing the double blow of a broken heart and a shattered arm.

As I began to lose my way once more, I started to read back over diary entries I had written when I was going through my first real episode of depression in 2011. I had started writing as a kind of therapy for some time before I reached out to the Gaelic Players Association for professional help.

Reading my own words from that spell was a stark reminder of the darkness I had endured. More importantly, it made me appreciate that I had emerged from it a stronger person and reminded me that I could do it again. I did think that if I'd read something like those diary entries during 2011, I would have been able to reach out for help so much sooner. I knew better than most that fighting the negativity inside me and lying to others about how I was feeling had been of little help.

I made a conscious decision to publish my reflections to help raise awareness of the issue of depression and mental health in Ireland. I knew the good it had the potential to do and the light I could shine, as a figure in Irish sport, on a topic that is so often stigmatised. Being honest, it felt more like something I had to do, something I felt bound to do, than something I chose. As I read my own raw and honest words it certainly gave me some perspective about my injury and bad luck, but it did not lift the dark cloud from over my head.

Struggling with the vacuum the injury had left in my weekly schedule, I foolishly decided to go on a complete bender in Dublin at the tail end of March, despite avoiding it since that miserable December night when I nearly ended my life. I was so fearful of the effect alcohol had on me that I even missed the night of celebration the DIT team had when they won the Sigerson Cup for the first time in its history.

I had been a selector for the team. The college had tried to get me back to do a master's so that I would be eligible to play that year. When I'd said that I was content with the job I had landed in Croke Park, they'd asked me to get involved on the management side of things, given that I knew the younger players coming through better than anyone else from coaching them at fresher level. I'd agreed to sign up, for two simple reasons: I enjoyed the managerial aspect of the game, and it reduced the amount of time I had to spend alone. It was another thing that could keep me busy.

After DIT's 3-09 to 0-08 victory over UCC in the final, the most successful day in the college's GAA history, the lads headed back to Dublin to celebrate their gallant march to glory, which included beating DCU in the semi-final and NUI Galway and NUI Maynooth in earlier rounds. They were an extremely talented group of footballers who had come together to produce a brand of exciting, attacking football combined with a mean defence that hadn't conceded a single goal throughout the competition.

While the lads were euphoric after their fantastic achievement and were ready to celebrate, I was flooded with doubt about joining them. I was friendly with plenty of the players, especially Monaghan's Colin Walshe and my fellow Cavan teammate Martin Reilly, and had both played with and managed some of the others over the previous couple of years. Naturally I wanted to revel in the victory but I was genuinely too scared to drink. As I zipped up the motorway I contemplated the pros and cons of joining the lads in the Boar's Head on Capel Street for the remainder of the night. I was far more aware of my relationship with alcohol than I had been, and had developed a more responsible attitude towards it, but I still had not achieved the understanding I needed in order to drink in peace without the fear of it yanking down on my mood.

Will I go on up and not drink?

Ah no, fuck that. I'm not standing around like a spare prick all night.

Sure, just call in and have a few, then. You can skip out early. You've put too much in over the years for DIT not to enjoy this with the boys.

But what if I get that urge again and do something stupid like jump in the Liffey?

You won't.

How do you know?

As I stewed on that question, I drove past an exit for Cavan on the M6. I felt selfish for even wanting to drink in that moment after the incident at Christmas, which was still my secret and my burden. Nobody knew how close I had come to leaving my family and friends behind that night.

I should have gone home. I don't trust myself to have just a few.

Fuck this. It's not worth the risk. I'll stay with my parents and be fresh for Cavan training. That's my priority.

I took the next exit, doubled back and spent the night alone in my bedroom. I hadn't wanted to risk being that close to the edge of the cliff again. I never got to see or touch the Sigerson Cup again after that.

Playing for Cavan gave me a natural excuse to avoid nights out with friends, and I was grateful to my sport for that. It says a lot about my state of mind after the arm break that I gave in to my self-imposed drinking ban to get a reprieve from what I was thinking and feeling. For one night, I drank and downed whatever I could get my hands on.

When I could squeeze no more in, I spent most of the night swinging my cast around the dance floor like a moron. It was complete escapism. I had grown weary of all the extra work depression was making me do – second-guessing myself all the time, trying to manage my emotions and how I appeared to others. I just wanted to get away from it all.

I woke up and had no idea how I had got home until a picture was uploaded onto Facebook of me getting food and then a taxi with a group of girls. Only then did I remember why I shouldn't drink when I feel so confused: my losing the run of myself was just me running away from my depression. I should have known better by that stage, but at least my night on the town reminded me that drink was not going to be the remedy. I knew what was required: it was back to counselling for me for another block of work with Niall. There was no fear whatsoever in calling for help when the black dog returned to follow me everywhere I went. After months of going it alone, I was heading back to that room – and when I got there I realised it wasn't a minute too soon.

There had been times earlier in the 2013 season when I considered booking an appointment, especially when I was tormented by so many doubts about my ability during those Down and Meath games, but I was reluctant to open myself up to the process again. That would have meant having to deal with the emotionally draining and thought-provoking experience of counselling while I was trying to function as an inter-county player. I was not sure I had the energy to do both to the standards I expected of myself, and I was happy to allow playing for Cavan to be a distraction from the other areas of my life that weighed down my mind.

I had foolishly and naively prioritised sporting ambitions ahead of my mental health but the break in my arm left me with no excuse to ignore what I knew I needed to do. In fact, it made me need it a whole lot more. I asked myself many times during those difficult weeks if football was worth all the hassle that it brought to my life given how it could pull on my mood so severely, mercilessly and swiftly.

The sessions helped to rebuild my resilience, and after a number of conversations with Niall I knew I wasn't going to let the depression control me again. I had learned too much and travelled too far down the path of recovery to let it consume me again.

It took every ounce of energy and willpower that I had to see the light at the end of the tunnel and to keep walking towards it. Having played in front of thousands of people in the previous weeks, having felt the positive surge that making those saves had brought me, it sickened me how easily my depression was able to drain me of optimism and joy. It sapped all my motivation and energy.

How fucking dare it do this to me again. Why would it drag me down like this when I've come so far?

After it was confirmed that my arm had been broken, Terry gave me some space before getting in touch again to encourage me to get back to football. Both he and the goalkeeping coach, Gary Rogers, unaware of the return of my depression, said the same thing. 'Make sure you stay involved. We have a long year ahead.'

They were two men I trusted, and I listened to them.

Gary was quick to emphasise that I might have a broken arm but I could still walk and run and train. I had a lot of time for him, and our relationship grew over the season, which was his first working with our county team. His sessions were the most innovative, demanding and enjoyable I experienced, as he was able to draw from his own training routine during back-to-back titles while playing soccer for Sligo Rovers and from time spent with Meath before his professional soccer career took off.

Even with the cast on my arm, the training was just what I needed at that time. When Gary had James Reilly and Conor Gilsenan – who had now been promoted to the senior ranks after the under-21 season had come to an end with a third consecutive Ulster title – doing drills, he worked them in a way that I could join in too. If the lads were catching the ball, I would either get an easy service that I could catch with one hand and throw back, or he would toss the ball in the air so I could punch it back with my left fist. The important thing was that on training nights I was covering every bit as much ground as the lads – often faster than they were. It kept me in shape and more importantly, sane.

I was able to really focus on my kick-outs too, and I made a lot of progress learning to shorten my run-up while maintaining accuracy and distance. Stephen Cluxton was my inspiration in that regard – the man had singlehandedly revolutionised the art of goalkeeping in Gaelic football and there was now more focus on the goalkeeper's role.

If I felt I was getting in the way at any stage I would go to the training field by myself with a number of balls and try to kick them into wheelie bins I'd placed in different key areas. It gave me real focus on improving the accuracy of my shorter kicks, as the players on our team were adamant that we improve that aspect of our game. We had made good progress against Meath and Monaghan but we struggled in the final league games against Fermanagh, Wicklow and Roscommon to win primary possession.

There is no denying that James was one of the finest goalkeepers for Cavan. I went to games as a youngster and had left in awe of the presence he had in the goals, and how he closed off angles to save so many shots from close range. However, the game had evolved beyond his style of goalkeeping; players now wanted a lower-trajectory pass that they could run on to rather than a long, high kick. They wanted to be able to turn and launch an attack quickly without having to contest with an opposition midfielder climbing up their back. I knew I could give them exactly that.

When either James or Conor was missing or injured, I would stand in goals for the training games, take the restarts and work as part of the group. Being able to talk and communicate to the lads was important; that is a big part of my game and it helped me feel appreciated, despite the cast on my arm. Obviously my shot-stopping ability was limited, but I felt like I was contributing.

As the weeks went on I grew in confidence again and I started throwing my body at shots. I dived a few times in drills too, although Gary told me to relax and not do anything stupid.

Throughout that period I kept telling myself I would be back in my jersey again and that I had to keep working hard and training.

'Coming out tomorrow?' asked my little brother Billy one evening in Dublin.

'I can't, lad. I've training tomorrow night.'

'What training?'

'Cavan training. I'm down the road to Breffni.'

'You have a broken arm, sure!' he said, with a bewildered look on his face.

'Wasn't I given two arms for a reason?' I said.

'You're mad.'

We left it at that. I was sitting in a room with five of my good friends, and from the looks on their faces they felt the same as my brother. They didn't understand. Plenty of people I knew questioned why I was still bothering to give football so much commitment and effort but I felt I had a point to prove to myself. I knew

I would regret it in later life if I didn't give myself the best chance possible to return to the team later in the season.

While all this was going on I had opened up and talked to two colleagues in the GAA, where I was still working as the National Social Media Coordinator, about going public with my story.

I appreciated that the first thing Alan Milton, Head of Media Relations, and Colin Regan, Community and Health Manager, were concerned about was my own wellbeing. All the questions they asked were about ensuring that I wasn't making a decision that I would regret later in life. They meant well, and were incredibly supportive friends, but their queries only made me more certain that I had to challenge the taboo in Ireland.

A meeting was set up with John Greene, the sports editor of the *Sunday Independent*, in which we would discuss publishing the story I had put together from all those thousands of words that my deeply depressed mind had conjured up on my laptop.

Familiar with the journalism world, I needed reassurances that a subeditor was not going to throw a nasty headline on an article that I had spent countless hours pouring my heart and soul into, trying my best to convey how confusing the experience of depression was for a young man in our society. My draft article that John read was 4,000 words, and I doubted whether a newspaper would be willing to offer up that space to one story. I was a young goalkeeper making his mark with Cavan, but I was no All-Ireland winner or even an established top-level player; I wouldn't have been known to the general public.

To my surprise he said the *Sunday Independent* would run my words verbatim. I would get PDF copies of the designed pages before they went to print so that I could show my immediate family what the finished article would look like; that way I could put their minds at ease, as well as my own. My family were incredibly supportive throughout the process and happily backed my decision to start a conversation in the national media.

With all that agreed upon, the big question looming was: when would it go to print? I was already 100 per cent certain that I wanted the story to be published, for two main reasons. I told myself that even if I only helped one person, if I could encourage one person to reach out for help and no longer suffer in silence, then it would all be worth it. I also wanted to do it because I felt like I was constantly walking around with a monkey on my back. I was spending time and energy hiding my secret from people, and I didn't want to have to do that anymore. It was like I was living in a constant web of lies. I had grown tired of keeping up the charade and trying to remember all the excuses and stories I'd made up.

Things had all come to a head one day while I was at work in Croke Park with the cast on my arm. Staring vacantly at the computer screen in front of me, I had this overwhelming urge to cry. All I could focus on were the waves of emotion as they rolled in. I could do nothing as I sat at my desk trying to keep it together.

My depression always seemed at its worst in the morning, but usually I could count on my sense of responsibility to the job to keep me in check and halt the slide downward. That day, though, I just knew I had to get out of there, especially after I'd imagined jumping off the sixth tier of the stadium. I had figured out by then that I could stop suicidal thoughts becoming suicidal feelings by choosing not to stew over them, choosing not to let them consume my train of thought. I went through phases of having suicidal thoughts even when I knew I wasn't suicidal. Simple as it sounds, this made me realise that not everything I thought about was true. A thought wasn't right or wrong, it just was – and I learned that I had some control over which thoughts became feelings and which feelings became actions.

With that knowledge, I could catch a suicidal thought before I reacted to it. I didn't have to feel guilty or angry for having a suicidal thought, and while I didn't fully understand why I was thinking them, I knew I didn't want those thoughts to gain a foothold as a feeling or, worse, an action.

However, that one particular moment stayed with me. I think it was because my brain had taken a place I worshipped so much – a historic stadium and my workplace – and turned it into a place where my life could end. It wasn't like the other times when I saw myself driving my car into a lake or swallowing a full box of tablets, and that fact turned my stomach. I needed to be alone and to concentrate in order to redirect the flow of my thoughts. I needed to hide from the world. I needed to let my guard down and let depression into my life. I could fight it all I liked, but I wasn't going to win that way. It was time to embrace my depression as a friend, ask it what it wanted and why it was here, rather than trying to fight it off like an enemy. I wanted a better understanding of why those suicidal thoughts kept turning up, rather than settling for any of the coping mechanisms I had been trying.

I went to the toilet and sat in a cubicle for a couple of minutes, again with tears in my eyes. It was like the 2011 nightclub experience when I frantically tried to make sense of my life and punched drunken notions into my phone. My head was all over the place. I eventually composed myself and walked into my boss's office.

'I need to go home,' I said. 'I'm after getting sick in the toilet there. Think I ate something funny last night.'

'Of course. That's no problem at all,' she replied.

That evening, while lying on my bed, I became angry and annoyed. I was pissed off that I had lied about how I was feeling and what I was going through. I promised myself that I would never lie again to cover up my depression. After all, how could I learn to live my life and accept the person I was if I was constantly hiding my feelings and being ashamed of what I was enduring? Like the young lads who had broken into the Cavan senior team earlier in the year and beaten Monaghan and Meath, I had to be the change that I wanted to see in my life.

A phone call from Terry Hyland three weeks before we were due to face Armagh in the opening round of the 2013 Ulster championship on 19 May had only added to my confusion. 'How's the arm feeling?' he asked.

'It's hard to know. I'm doing all I can to get back as soon as possible, but it's frustrating the life out of me,' I replied. I said nothing about the return of my depression.

'Good man. The reason I'm asking is because if you are fit to play, then I still see you in our plans for the Armagh game,' he said.

I nearly dropped the phone when I heard those words. I stared at the cast that was still on my arm. My confidence that I could recover in time to make the team had been dwindling, but he still clearly believed in my ability and what I could bring to the pitch – and that meant a lot.

I wanted to make my senior Ulster championship debut more than anything in the world, even if it meant risking long-term damage to my arm or wrist. I was willing to risk it so that I could play again for Cavan. I desperately wanted to run out in front of the crowd and rediscover the happy place that the save against Sligo had taken me to. It was the easiest way to escape from all the drivel in my head. I didn't stop for one second to think about the anxiety and uncertainty that could come with returning to the team. I saw the prize dangled in front of me, and I wanted it.

Terry knew how hard I had worked for the opportunity, despite the setback with my arm. I will always appreciate that vote of confidence he gave me. The Antrim experience, when he chose James over me, seemed a lifetime ago. I felt I had earned his trust again. He wanted me in the team and was strongly considering taking a gamble on me if I could prove my fitness. It was a timely reminder of the progress I had made.

I always knew it would be tight, time-wise, to get game-ready, so I pushed hard. It was my ability to ensure we retained possession on our own kick-outs that had me in contention. My kick was more reliable and consistent than either Conor's or James's and I knew the lads involved in the middle section of the field, like Gearoid McKiernan and David Givney, preferred me slinging it out to them.

'Look, Terry, you know me well enough at this stage. I want to play so badly. I'm not sure where exactly things are with my arm at the minute, but all I can say is that I will do everything I can to make it back in time,' I said passionately.

The problem was that the team physio, Simon Gaffney, and the team doctor were pessimistic. Both felt the timeline was too tight, given the damage and the nature of wrist injuries, as there are so many bones and tendons interlinked in such a small area. The ignorance of my youth, however, chose to ignore them both.

With plans coming together for my article, Terry had given me a glimmer of hope that maybe my season wasn't over. Could I actually do it? Could I get back in time for the Armagh game?

We were due to play Meath on 3 May as we fine-tuned our game, and realistically I needed to play against them if I was going to start in the big one 16 days later. My cast had only come off late the previous week and the physio maintained that I wasn't ready for competitive action. When I demanded that he strap up the wrist heavily so I could play in an in-house match in Mullagh immediately afterwards, he rolled his eyes in bemusement.

I didn't want to hear what he had to say if it wasn't good news. The irony of it, given I was regularly getting lost in a world of my own negativity. Denial is a powerful force in competitive sport. At times you have no choice but to employ it if you want to overcome niggling injuries and the many self-doubts they cause, and I knew that better than most.

I made a deal with the physio that I would get one final X-ray before the Meath game. I was given a last-minute appointment and I went to learn my fate on the Friday in the Sports Surgery Clinic in Santry – the place where Enda had given me so much inspiration and guidance back in 2010. As I came to a halt in the underground car park I decided that if the bones in my wrist were healed from a medical point of view, I would play later that evening against the Royals, regardless of the pain it would bring. If they weren't, then I would back down and swallow my pride.

As it turned out, I had already trained on a wrist that was still damaged. My dream was over. That was the final nail in the coffin. When the doctor left the room for a minute I took out my phone and took a picture of my X-rayed arm on the screen. The crack in one bone was clearly visible to the naked eye and there was a chipped bone that hadn't fully knitted back together. The truth hurt. I felt the tears in my eyes as the conversation with Terry telling me I was in his plans replayed in my mind.

I took the picture so that I'd have a reminder of why I wasn't out on the field in the ensuing weeks, a reminder of just how serious the situation was. I accepted that my body needed more time to heal, and took a back seat as the lads went into full championship mode.

With my playing destiny out of my hands, I made the decision to publish the article about my experience with depression the Sunday after the Cavan–Armagh game. I very much wanted to publish it sooner, and it was something I needed to do to liberate myself, but I didn't want to distract the management or players in the build-up to our biggest game of the year. I sat in the stand in Kingspan Breffni Park, along with

Gearoid, who had unfortunately torn his cruciate in a club game, and watched as we beat Armagh by 1-15 to 1-11.

I had worked under Terry Hyland, Anthony Forde, Joe McCarthy and Padraig Dolan for a number of years, but I honestly don't think a Cavan team was ever as prepared as our group was for that game. The regular supporters had no idea how hard that management team had worked behind the scenes to give the players the best possible chance of executing an optimum performance. They were unbelievably meticulous.

Joe's analysis of the opposition was like nothing I had seen before. The level of detail in his report on Armagh was simply extraordinary; there were professional teams that came nowhere near the standards he set. Gary Rogers confirmed this when I had asked him about the level of analysis he had seen in dressing rooms throughout his professional soccer career. Joe highlighted common patterns in their play under Paul Grimley – how they liked to press high, and the specific areas they liked to work the ball to. It was fascinating. For the first time in my life I felt the GAA world had caught up with the fantasy realm of Football Manager, an unbelievably detailed computer game I spent many hours playing. While I was in charge of a fantasy club, the game gave a full scouting department that would report back to me on future opposition and players so that I could alter my own team and tactical setup accordingly.

We had watched highlights of Armagh's league games to back up Joe's case, and the space they left at the back was astonishing. If we moved the ball quickly and got possession past their initial high defensive line, it was clear there would be acres of space to exploit. We had also devised a plan for Alan Clarke to double up as a sweeper and a second man-marker on their star forward, Jamie Clarke. 'Toasty' is the best man that I have played with to work the sweeper role. His defensive positioning, awareness and game intelligence are just top-notch – he is a proper old-school, no-nonsense defender.

All in all the win was an excellent day's work, and a big scalp for us to take. It was another signal of intent; a warning to the other teams that this was a new Cavan team without the baggage of previous years.

Management also gave a debut to Conor Gilsenan in goals, and he had as solid an afternoon as he could have hoped for. There was nothing he could do about the goal and was very assured with several balls that dropped short. I had known Conor from our Bailieborough days, and I was delighted that he had grabbed his opportunity with both hands. Of course I was jealous too, in the circumstances, but that was life. He got an opportunity and he took it.

The following morning, with the dust settling on our biggest championship win in years, I called Terry from the car park in Croke Park and told him about my plans with the *Sunday Independent* as the article was to appear six days later.

At 9.45 that morning I followed up our conversation with an email that had the full article attached. I wanted him to be aware of the situation, but I also wanted his blessing to go forward with it. Even though it was something I felt a strong need to do, I still had a few niggling doubts about whether an inter-county player could come out publicly with something as stigmatised as a mental-health struggle.

I had explained to him my reasons for doing it during our phone call and I had got the thumbs up that I'd wanted. Again, there was no long, deep, meaningful conversation between us, but it was honest and to the point – just how I liked it. After taking time to read the article later on, Terry called me back, congratulated me on a brave piece of writing, and admitted how he wasn't sure he would have known how to deal with a player in relation to such a sensitive issue. We had a laugh over the fact that at least he did now.

'You don't have to know all the answers for them, that's the beauty of it. You just have to know where help is available and get them to it,' I said.

With that worry out of the way, the next thing I had to do was tell the lads on the team, as I didn't want them getting a surprise reading about it in the paper when we were in the middle of a championship campaign. I kept it short and sweet with a message posted on the team's Facebook page explaining that I had a piece coming out that weekend about a difficult time that I had gone through. If anybody had any grievances about it, they never said, as I got nothing but support from my teammates. I felt the family atmosphere had really grown within the team, and although we only had one win under our belts in the preliminary round of the Ulster championship, the progress we had made in terms of attitude, spirit and togetherness was huge when compared with previous regimes I'd been part of.

On 26 May, 4,000 of my finest words explaining how I went from playing for Cavan in an All-Ireland under-21 final in Croke Park to considering crashing my car into a wall in just six months were printed in the *Sunday Independent*. From there it was posted on GAA.ie, the GPA website and later on thejournal.ie.

I knew it was going to get attention, but hadn't realised just how much. Players I had huge respect for, like Oisín McConville and Niall McNamee, had gone public about gambling addictions in previous years and had really shone a light on that topic, while Donal Óg Cusack had done tremendous work to open up conversations for the LGBT community. Dublin's Dessie Farrell had also talked about his own struggles in his book *Tangled Up in Blue* after he retired, but by 2013 no active player had really tackled depression head on.

The article went viral and was viewed hundreds of thousands of times online alone, not to mention the newspaper circulation, which stands at over 200,000 copies per week. Messages of support arrived in their hundreds via phone, text, Twitter, Facebook, emails and letters. Most were from close to home but others were from complete strangers who got in touch from as far away as Australia, the US and Canada. Media requests came in quickly too, from local radio stations like Northern Sound in Cavan, all the way up to RTÉ's *Saturday Night with Miriam*, hosted by Miriam O'Callaghan.

I was very careful with the media appearances that I chose to do. I just wanted people to read the piece, not for me to talk about it repeatedly. My colleague Alan Milton, the GAA's Head of Media Relations, was an unbelievable help dealing with that influx of requests and came as close as I will ever get to my own Jerry-Maguire-style agent.

The compassion of the Irish people truly blew me away. When I made the decision to publish that piece it was because it had dawned on me that I was not the only one suffering with an illness that did its very best to make every fibre of your being feel that you were completely and utterly alone in your struggle. I wanted to reach out, to highlight the issue, and hopefully help somebody else in a difficult place.

In the aftermath of the article I was amazed by the sheer number of people who told me that depression had touched their lives directly or indirectly. I couldn't believe that I had once thought that I was the only person in the world to feel the way I had. Even a close friend admitted to me that they had been to counselling before but had kept it a secret from everyone.

Clearly I had achieved what I had set out to do; I had started conversations, and that one with my close friend left a lasting impression. I couldn't believe that we had both worked so hard to keep our experiences with counselling a secret; it was just another example of the stigma that existed in our society. It felt even more ridiculous when we realised how supportive we could have been to each other through the turbulent times we had faced. I knew I needed to have more real talks and meaningful conversations with those I trusted.

There were plenty more twists and turns in the recovery of both my mind and body, but being honest about my experiences released me from so much of the baggage that I was carrying within me. The truth had set me free.

11
The Debut

The first few weeks after I had published the article about my experiences with depression went by in a blur.

Doing media interviews on shows such as Newstalk's *Off the Ball* with the brilliant Ger Gilroy turned out to be extremely therapeutic for me. Having spent so long musing over my words on paper, it was empowering to say them out loud for all to hear. It was another step in my recovery and rehabilitation.

The interviews were nothing like the ones so often carried out at a sports press launch when I would be either speaking for the team or just after a match. Though they were open and honest discussions about my depression, they were very much consigned to that spell in 2011 when I had faced up to depression for the first time. I did not open up or discuss my more recent struggles, even though there were plenty to choose from. Perhaps it was easier to talk about past depression, when a bit of distance could give me some perspective.

For the interview with Ger Gilroy, I sat nervously on my chair in the studio as he introduced me. I had no idea of the twists and turns that our conversation would take.

'I wanted to ask you first about the reaction, because honestly I can't remember such a spontaneous outpouring from the GAA community – and indeed the wider community at large – for an autobiographical piece. Did it surprise you?' he asked.

'Yeah, I suppose I was surprised by how willing people have been to open up to me. I don't want to go into specifics, but one girl really opened up to me about a family member and asked what she could do to help him. She was just so grateful for the reply. And some of the stuff I got really was quite moving.'

'There is a sense that part of this might become part of your life's work. You are young, and I don't want to pigeonhole you for the rest of your life, but it's rare enough that we have an open discourse about mental health, and you are somebody who has actually written it down in cold black and white, and it has gone around the world online. Is that something you might be interested in? Being an advocate for better mental health in Ireland?'

It all came tumbling out effortlessly over the 30-minute conversation between us. To this day I feel it was the best interview I have given, and that was in large part thanks to the excellent interviewer. It was funny to think how far my piece had travelled too. Alistair Campbell, Tony Blair's one-time high-profile PR guru in the UK, who had also worked with the British and Irish Lions, shared my piece to his 300,000-plus Twitter followers, as he is a major mental-health advocate in the UK.

While I was relatively comfortable talking about my experiences publicly like that, it was important to stress to people listening, who may have been going through a difficult time, that all they needed to do to start their recovery was to tell one person whom they trusted in order to reach out for help. They didn't need to shout it from the rooftops for all to hear.

Delighted with the good I felt I had done and the awareness I had raised around the issue of mental health in modern society, I wanted to go back to focusing on football in the short term. I really hoped to become first-choice goalkeeper for Cavan again. When I had achieved that, I would dedicate more time to getting involved in mental health work. My initial calling to publish the piece had been met, but I knew from the outset that it was not a drum I could stop banging.

~

I still felt my broken arm was preventing me from getting back on the field, as it had to be heavily strapped to ensure it could withstand the pressure of stopping a shot. There were times at training when I struggled to get my gloves on because the bandaging increased the size of my hand so much. My gloves kept bursting at the seam below the fingers due to the bulk of my hand, and I might not have been able to afford my car loan that month if it wasn't for Gary Rogers and Atak Sports, who kindly supplied gloves, which cost €50 a pair, free of charge. There was no denying that the flexibility and mobility of my hand was restricted. More worryingly, I felt I was dropping balls, particularly ones coming in from a height, which normally I could hold on to. The rigid strapping was designed to stop my hand bending backwards, so when I went to soften my hands to embrace the ball, I couldn't – my hand was like a mini brick wall, and the ball kept rebounding.

At a time when I needed my confidence back quickly, my wrist was constantly gnawing at me and planting more doubts. I kept going, determined I would overcome them and put myself in contention for a place in the starting fifteen. I had successfully come through worse uncertainties earlier in the year, so I was adamant that I could do it again.

I appeared in the Cavan jersey for the first time since going public with my story against Louth in the Leinster junior championship – 11 days after the Armagh game. I got through that one without any hiccups, but we lost a tight contest in the next round to Longford. I was happy with a clean sheet and the fact that I only got one sharp jolt of pain in my wrist during the match.

Things continued on the up when I was chosen to start against the previous year's All-Ireland finalists, Mayo, on the June bank holiday Monday in Ballina, as Conor Gilsenan was on a holiday he had booked before joining the senior panel midway through the season.

'We might be up against it around midfield a bit today, so if the short kick-out is on, go for it,' said Terry after strolling up to me during the warm-up.

I knew I couldn't play it safe; this was a serious opportunity for me, so I just went for broke. I was all in. My kicks worked a treat and we orchestrated passes into space really well. Ronan Flanagan, one of the most intelligent footballers ever to wear the Cavan jersey, and Alan Clarke took on most of the responsibility after we had a quick discussion before throw-in about Terry's preference to go short on the day. They knew I would be looking for them with quick restarts.

Along with Rory Dunne, who was back from injury, Ronan and Alan constantly looked for the ball in our own defence, when the easy option would have been to hide behind their man and let me punt it out to midfield. It was a good choice, because that day it was a battle we were likely to lose. I took chances and squeezed balls past outstretched Mayo hands. At the break, we were in the lead by two points, 0-10 to 1-5. We had implemented our style and game plan on a strong Mayo team that featured the likes of All-Star Andy Moran, Aidan O'Shea, Kevin McLoughlin and Donal Vaughan. It was another boost to the notion that we were slowly transforming into a formidable outfit that could compete with the best around.

I knew before the game that I was only going to get the first half, which is probably why I was so certain I needed to put my stamp on things early on. The game was going so well, I was frustrated at having to step aside, but at least I got to relax after putting in a strong performance I could be proud of. I also got the chance to see what my rival had up his sleeve.

There were wholesale changes on our side at the break, when James Reilly came in for me. Mayo took complete control of the game as our second 15 never really got going. They choked us at midfield and hammered five goals into our net. On the bus journey home, I was certain that I was once again ahead of James in the pecking order. One down, one to go.

I sat on the substitutes' bench as we beat Fermanagh to qualify for the last four in Ulster and remained there for the semi-final against Monaghan. With the increased focus from our team on retaining possession from restarts, Conor's kick was intercepted down the middle and Christopher McGuinness found himself clean through. He kept his cool, and rolled it into the net. It was a devastating defeat for us, losing out 1-10 to 0-12. We had come so agonisingly close to qualifying for an Ulster final, when recent years for us had involved so many embarrassing defeats and let-downs.

We bounced back against Fermanagh in the qualifiers, though, and just as my patience with being an understudy was wearing thin, the rollercoaster took another unexpected turn. I had spent the journey to training one night in the car with Padraic Reilly bemoaning the life of an inter-county panel member who isn't getting game time. We both agreed it is one of the hardest slogs on the GAA circuit.

'As bad as you think you are, lad, trying being the sub-keeper. Basically I'm not getting on that field unless Conor gets injured or sent off. And I am pretty sure the keeper would have to pull a gun out of his sock and shoot somebody to actually get a red card in GAA. At least you have a chance of coming on if someone isn't playing well. And sure, if you take your opportunity and make the most of it when it comes, then you have a good chance of starting the next day,' I told him.

Both of us were working in Dublin, as were a few others on the panel. Each week, we gave up our Monday evening to meet up and do gym work together, and we travelled to Cavan on Wednesdays. I'd get to my desk for 9 a.m. and leave at 5 p.m. sharp to hit the road. I'd get back to my bed at around midnight. Depending on work, I could either travel home on the Friday evening and stay with my parents all weekend to make getting to the game easier, or travel up and down again. Either way, the schedule made for a lot of travel and many long days.

'Podge, do you ever ask yourself if this is all worth it?' I wondered as we drove down the M3 motorway towards Kingspan Breffni Park.

'Yeah, of course I do. It's a bit different for me now than when I was in college, all I really thought about then was playing football. I'm busy with work at the minute and can't go on some business trips and other things because of the commitment here. From experience, the best thing I can tell you is to not worry about any of that now. Think about it more at the end of the year. We're in the middle of the championship, and you never know what will happen,' he said.

As panel members, we obviously wanted the team to thrive, but we had to have a selfish streak that demanded we get our day on the battlefield. The lads who were starting in our places fed off that feistiness in us too, because knowing we were chomping at the bit pushed them on and stopped them sliding into the comfort zone. I could never understand the mindset of players who were just happy to turn up week in, week out and not really push for a starting place. I mean, go do something else with your life! Being a substitute drove me crazy.

Thanks to my performances in training, I felt I was narrowing the gap all the time on Conor in the build-up to the next qualifier game against Derry, but I also knew that Terry wasn't just going to change goalkeeper on a whim; few managers do. I knew his hand would probably have to be forced.

Training had finished on the Wednesday night before the Derry match and I spent a few extra minutes practising kick-outs with Conor and the midfielders. When I left the field, there was still a group of them working on frees, shots and penalties.

Back in the dressing room, I peeled layer after layer of strapping off my wrist and got ready to hit the shower. As I walked towards the showers, word came in that Conor was after going down in a heap. He had jumped up to catch a ball dropping in and had landed his foot on a rolling ball that had come from elsewhere. Just like that, he was out and I was in.

Obviously I felt sorry for him as he sat in the corner of the dressing room with ice on his ankle, but inside I couldn't help but be ecstatic. Only I knew everything I had gone through over the previous two years, and now all the sacrifices, struggles and doubts seemed worth it: I had my chance to start a championship match. I sat upstairs having something to eat with some of the boys, and when Conor's injury came up in conversation I tried to play it cool.

'He has a few more days to rest it, so we'll just wait and see,' I said calmly as I forked some pasta into my mouth. Conor and myself were friendly, but this was the heartbreak side of what we'd signed up for – especially as net-minders – and I knew that better than anyone.

James had left the panel, so it was just down to the two of us now; one man's misery was going to be the other's good luck, pure and simple.

I reminded myself that he only got into the team in the first place because I had broken my arm. I was 100 per cent certain that if I had not sustained that injury back in March, I would have started every game for the rest of the season because of the progress I was making.

Conor and I brought out the best of each other in training that summer, and there was good chemistry between the two of us and Gary Rogers. He was better under a high ball than me, but I had a superior kick-out, so we were constantly trying to improve our weaknesses and boost our strengths to get ahead of one another.

We were pushed hard too by Rogers, who became an excellent mentor. All I had worked for, all the sacrifices, the counselling, the tears, the anger, the broken bones, the frustration, the joy – everything was finally leading to the opportunity that I had now been given. I tried to forget about the history of it all and focus on my own performance – I needed to put in a strong one against Derry and get over the doubts. After months on the rollercoaster, my fate was now in my own hands once again.

Padraic looked at me in the car as we pulled out of Kingspan Breffni Park to head back to Dublin. All I could do was smile and shrug my shoulders. 'And me after moaning the whole way down!' I said.

~

On a scorching hot 20 July in Celtic Park I made my senior championship debut for Cavan. It was everything I thought it would be and more. I had officially come back from the brink.

I couldn't catch my breath in the warm-up and I felt completely exhausted, almost as if I was going to get sick. But incredibly, the voice that had troubled me before the Meath game back in February never made a comeback – these were the good type of nerves. I just wanted the referee to throw in the ball so I could finally allow myself to smile and be proud of what I had overcome to be standing there in between those posts. I knew I had earned it. My nerves settled down as the national anthem played and I soaked up the championship atmosphere.

In the first half, I put two kick-outs straight over the sideline on the stand side of the ground. I attempted to force the ball into a pocket of space that simply wasn't there. I could hear the crowd moan as the ball bounced out of bounds. It didn't bother me though, and even when the other voice tried to chip in, I quickly shut it out.

As Derry lined up a free, I closed my eyes and imagined where I was putting the next kick-out. Instead of visualising all the bodies running around the pitch, I focused on the wheelie bin that my imagination had placed neatly on an immaculately clear pitch, remembering how I used to sharpen my accuracy on the training field by myself. As David Givney jogged back out for the restart, I told him exactly where I was putting it. He caught it and ran down the field to work a score.

'Great kick. That's your score,' said Rory Dunne.

I gave him a nod of approval. 'Man up again, lads. Get ready for the next ball,' I roared.

That longer kick settled me down and I went back to the short kick-outs that we had talked about and worked on in training. I even hit two off my left foot, which was my weaker side, all the way out to Killian Clarke on the right side of the field, such was the confidence I was feeling. A gang behind the goals noticed it too and started chanting my name to a beat. 'Alan O'Mara,' they shouted, as one banged a drum after each call.

As the clock ticked over into injury time, Derry took the lead by a point, 0-18 to 0-17, after Mark Lynch slotted over a free. Before he'd struck it, Rory had turned to me on the line and said, 'Make sure you have a ball ready to go, O'Mara.'

'One step ahead of you, lad. Just get out of the 21 as quick as you can and bring the rest with you,' I replied confidently.

As soon as the ball went between the posts, I had the new ball in my hands and sprinted out to put it on the tee. I looked up and saw Martin Reilly with some space in front of him on my left wing. All I did was call out one simple word. 'Marty!'

When he took a step towards it, I zipped the ball in his direction and it landed straight in his hands. It felt telepathic. Pound for pound, he is one of the best footballers I have ever seen and one of the most underrated players in the country.

We broke at speed up the pitch in the final minute of the match as Derry tried desperately to race back and crowd out the scoring zone, but the end result was Damien O'Reilly curling over a left-footed point under pressure. Derry had been absolutely certain they had the game won, but they were the latest side to find out the hard way that we weren't the Cavan team of previous years. I could just see the energy and spirit drain from their bodies as the referee blew the final whistle.

The atmosphere I felt as we huddled under the stand waiting for a further 20 minutes of extra time was astonishing. I didn't want it to end. I would have played for another ten hours if they'd wanted me to. I got flashbacks to the under-21 campaign of 2011. I didn't doubt the team or myself. Instead I simply got the feeling that it was going to be our day.

We won the game with six points to spare thanks to the fresh blood brought in, including more young guns like Michael Argue, another clubmate of mine who had made his debut the same day as me, and Dara McVeety – they got four points from play between them. I had coached Michael for the local soccer and GAA teams when he was younger and it was great to be able to share that day together.

The next weekend, we were paired against London, who were the beaten Connacht finalists. They were on the crest of a wave but we knew we had to back up the Derry scalp with another big performance, especially as the game had been scheduled for Croke Park as part of a triple-header.

I was definitely more nervous than I had been for my debut. Since breaking my arm in the Sligo game, I wasn't dealing with high balls confidently. Part of that was because of the physical state of my wrist. Sometimes when the ball connected with my hand I would get a sharp jolt of pain. But the real problem was a mental one, as I kept second-guessing myself and questioning my ability to cope with the dropping ball, despite the fact that I contested one with Derry's Eoin Bradley right at the death and got a solid fist to it.

London scored a goal in the 20th minute after Paul Geraghty out-jumped Rory Dunne on the edge of the square to slap home a pass from the left side of the goals. Initially I was just annoyed and told myself that I should have got it. I felt responsible for the goal, and all of a sudden the voice in my head started to have a field day, telling me I wasn't fit to be in Ireland's best stadium.

Against Derry I had got lost in the moment and had felt like the old me, but it didn't take much on this day to get me back to overthinking everything and beating myself up about it throughout the remainder of the game. It was a far cry from my earlier, pre-depression seasons when I was always adamant that the bigger the day, the better I would play. I couldn't keep it quiet, so I focused on my kicking game instead – that was an area in which I still had supreme confidence.

The perspective I got from being in the towering stadium made it easier to see our blue jerseys and where exactly the space was. I pinged balls around the field like I was Stephen Cluxton, and it felt incredible. I was playing more like a quarter-back than a keeper, and rather than launching long kicks down the field, I was sailing balls out to Givney, Cian Mackey, Martin Reilly and Fergal Flanagan, who were bursting into the vacant areas of the field, leaving their men behind them. They had complete trust that I would land the ball in their arms.

I decided to execute a kick-out I had been working on while my arm was broken, where I would put the ball on the tee and stand perpendicular to midfield. I would then take one step back and curl a side-foot-style banana kick, like a David Beckham soccer free-kick, around the arms of the corner-forward and land it just on the inside of the right sideline between the 45-metre and 21-metre lines.

Most goalkeepers dink it over the arms of the forwards, but the trouble with that is that the higher the ball travels, the longer it takes to come down and into my target's hands, and the more likely we'd lose possession. My new technique meant that the ball bounced off the grass and into their hands, and it was a kick Cian Mackey in particular loved to run onto. We never really talked about it much, but I had sent it to him once that way and from then on, whether it was in training or a game, he kept coming looking for it.

There was no way I would have tried it back in January when my confidence was much lower. One slight miscalculation meant it would go straight to the corner-forward to kick the ball into an empty net. The voice in my head constantly warned me to play it safe but I kept pushing myself to the edge. I had to trust that all the work I had done in the previous months would get me where I needed to be; otherwise it would all have been for nothing.

After the London game, Padraig Dolan, the team's video analyst, gave me a further confidence boost as I stewed over the return of the voice in my head throughout the match. 'That was one of the best kicking performances I have ever seen in Croke Park. I really mean that. You were exceptional,' he said.

I was delighted to hear that as I was getting on the bus to head home. My mood was lifted even further when I thought of the excellent save I made at the end of the second half. I had raced off my line to close the angle on the oncoming Damien Dunleavy and thrown my heavily bandaged right hand directly in the way of the shot without a second's hesitation.

It was just a reflex, as most of my best saves were. For a man constantly thinking about everything and anything, that was one part of goalkeeping I loved – those moments when I did something without realising it and let my training and experience take over. Goalkeeping drove me mad at times but it also offered me those little avenues of escape.

I felt nothing but the hairs standing up on the back

of my neck and sheer exhilaration as I thought of my parents sitting in the Hogan Stand smiling with pride. It got even better when we picked up the rebound, ran the length of the Croke Park pitch and got a goal of our own through Niall McDermott to see off London by 1-17 to 1-08.

Despite the positive feedback, the goal we conceded was still bothering me, and in my mind it came to overpower all the good things I had done in the match. I think it was a lingering effect of my depression; part of my brain was still constantly scanning for ways to put me down and hold me back.

If I were a beach ball, depression just wanted to grab me, pull me underwater and keep me there, even though that wasn't my natural state. I longed to burst out of the water and rise into to air so everybody in Croke Park could see how good a player I still was, how the depression couldn't keep me down, but I felt trapped between those two states for 70 minutes.

When I got home, I watched the goal back several times on the TV, and immediately felt I had been way too harsh on myself in the moment. I needed to stop letting the negative voice distract me and get back to focusing on the next ball immediately. I used to be so good at it naturally, so it was a skill I had completely taken for granted and I had to figure out how to reclaim it.

The pass which led to the London goal had come from a forward who crossed it, almost soccer style, from about 20 yards to the left of the goals and eight or nine yards from the end line. Because of the low trajectory of the pass, my starting position needed to have been about three yards off the goal line to give me a realistic chance of diving out and punching the ball clear before it reached its target. However, if I had taken those steps in anticipation then I would have left the entire near-post area of the goals wide open for the forward to score. Even if I had time to calculate all that, though, I never would have taken the gamble. There is no doubt that the best goalkeepers are wired differently to most other players – but we often forget that not all goals can be stopped, as much as we might like to think otherwise.

The voice tried to tell me that I was simply making excuses for myself. So after studying the footage for hours I asked Gary to check it out without telling him my feelings on it. He came back with similar thoughts, and said his opinion was shared by the team management. I knew I was overanalysing it. I stopped looking at the goal they scored and fast-forwarded it to my save. I was delighted to see it again, and annoyed that I had let my negative thoughts force me to watch the London goal for so long.

I snapped.

'When will this thing ever fuck off!' I said out loud as I slammed my fist into the chair in our sitting room. Nobody else was around to hear my outburst. I didn't want to be the beach ball anymore, being held underwater against its will. Psychologically, I was still scarred from the Sligo incident back in March and my depression was feeding from that. I had just one more week to build up resilience because I was about to face the biggest test of my career.

We were returning to Croke Park on 4 August to play an All-Ireland quarter-final against a Kerry team that featured the likes of Tomás Ó Sé, Paul Galvin, Kieran Donaghy, Darran O'Sullivan, Colm Cooper, James O'Donoghue and Declan O'Sullivan.

12
The Kingdom

In the aftermath of any championship defeat, somebody invariably tried to tell me that 'there's always next year'. Parents say it to console their children, partners say it in a desperate attempt to cheer up their opposite half and work colleagues say it to end awkward silences at the water cooler.

Those people always mean well but they never realise just how far off next year seems after a painful exit with Cavan. When I wear my tribe's colours, when I put myself out there to be judged, football becomes a lot more than a game to me. It dominates my thoughts. It becomes a way of life. I drive hundreds of miles a week just to be part of it, to feel how it makes me feel. I travel, I train, I rest and I recover on a loop for a whole year. I organise the rest of my life around football, and it has been that way for as long as I can remember. I do all that because I can't wait for the next emotional high, the sense of fulfilment and accomplishment that achieving something

188

with others brings to my life. Winning as a team and having a sense of belonging is important to me.

Travelling together for big matches is when I feel the bond with my team most strongly. In my own little way, I know I am heading off to war with my men, and certain lads would trigger different memories of battles we'd fought in the past. I felt that sensation so strongly on the way to Croke Park to take on Kerry in the last eight of the All-Ireland series.

Gearoid McKiernan reminded me of all the injuries I had overcome to be on the bus; Jack Brady of all the travelling I had done just to earn my seat. Niall McDermott had been there for all the gym sessions that I'd endured in an effort to claim my place. Oisin Minagh made me think of the years I'd spent dreaming about just getting on this bus in the first place.

On 4 August 2013 I wouldn't have traded my seat there for anywhere else in the world. It was what I had dreamed about for so many years – playing with Cavan at the top level and competing against the best teams in the country. We were now far from being the laughing stock of past years.

On the way in to the game, I saw our smiling supporters. Grown men in blue jerseys jumped up and down, waving to our team when they saw the steel horse coming. Children sprinted along trying to keep up with the bus, eager to get a glimpse of the lucky souls who would emerge from the bowels of Croke Park in a little over an hour to fight their way to the top like gladiators. We had the chance to bring joy to the faces of the thousands who had travelled from the Breffni County.

Cavan–Kerry was a rivalry that went back a long way, and was most famous for the battle of the Polo Grounds, New York in 1947 – the only time the All-Ireland final was played outside of Ireland. GAA officials in New York had grown increasingly concerned about the dwindling interest in Gaelic games and felt a glamorous event would win back supporters. After much debate it was decided that the '47 final would take place across the Atlantic, and Cavan won by 2-11 to 2-7, arguably the county's most famous win.

Fifty years later, the counties duelled again when the last Cavan team to win the Ulster senior title were beaten by the green and gold.

Now it was our turn to make history as the rivalry continued, and as I prepared for the battle ahead, I soaked it all up. The hormones and adrenalin built up in my body, slowly starting to vibrate in the pit of my stomach like a small tremor before a more powerful earthquake. The closer we got to the stadium, the slower the bus travelled as the crowd congested. People stared through the windows at us and I stared back. I knew that this bus was the place to be, and I knew so many of them would love to be on it with me. The bus was a sign to them that their army had arrived. It was more than just a game, it was a pilgrimage.

For me and the fans alike, the venue is a magical place. But as I travelled to the game, Croke Park also brought me back to some of my darkest moments, like resisting the urge to cry at my desk when my depression was at its worst. This time, however, the flashbacks didn't upset me at all; instead, they made me realise how far I had travelled down the path of what had become an increasingly enlightening journey. More than anything, I was proud to be back in Croke Park and starting on a Cavan team that was looking to reach an All-Ireland semi-final for the first time since 1997, when twice in recent years I had gone worryingly close to ending my life.

My depression had made the highs less enjoyable and the lows more torturous. Even when things did go well, I was just glad they hadn't gone badly rather than enjoying the moment in a positive frame of mind. It was relief more than pleasure. And now, instead of embracing death like that little voice in my head had wanted me to, I was buzzing with life on the inside. I was nervous, I was excited and I was dreading it all at the same time. It was invigorating, and felt healthy and positive.

The overwhelming emotions that had frustrated me so much now confirmed something really, really important to me: I was alive. I was chasing the dream of my youth. I had promised myself that I wouldn't let depression take that from me, and it hadn't. As the bus rolled through Ballybough and towards the Cusack Stand entrance, I caught a glimpse of the mighty arena soaring above the cover of the surrounding houses and flats. I allowed myself a short, satisfied smile.

I thought of Niall and the room where I had learned so much about myself as a person and depression in general. It was only a couple of hundred yards back up the main Drumcondra Road, but in the grand scheme of things, I knew I had travelled much farther than that.

~

Only one team can be crowned All-Ireland champions, and the rest have to endure the torture chamber that is a defeated championship dressing room. Unfortunately, our exit came at the hands of Kerry in a game where a lacklustre first half cost us dearly. We went in trailing by 0-11 to 0-2. 'All right, lads, sit down. There is no point dressing it up, it hasn't happened for us in that half. I'd be the first to hold my hands up and say that maybe we went in wrong with the change of system. We're going to push a man on now in this half because we have to go after it. This game is not over,' said Terry Hyland.

The dressing room was awash with frustration, anger and disappointment. Every single one of us knew we had not performed anywhere close to the level that we expected of ourselves. Some players had gone quiet, while others like Mossy Corr, Rory Dunne and Alan Clarke were talking out loud to pep things up. They were adamant that we had a lot more to give, and that we must go out and do just that in the second half.

I was caught between those two mindsets. I was like a turtle, unsure of whether to stick my head out and be noticed or withdraw to the comfort of my shell.

Screw it, Alan. We've come this far. 'This is not over, boys! We have another half to go. We can't let the year end like this,' I said.

We threw caution to the wind after the restart and drove at them with purpose. We chased them down and outscored them by three points to win the second half, but by then the damage was done. Kerry never looked overly worried and saw the game out in third gear. We exited the championship by 0-15 to 0-9 with nothing but a bagful of regrets.

When the final whistle sounded, I exited the field looking at my feet, but was stopped on the way by some opposing players who wished to express their sympathies. I managed to conjure up a word for Darran O'Sullivan, whom I knew from DIT as I'd been was a selector on the Sigerson Cup-winning team he played on earlier in the year. We'd sat together on the bus for the semi-final and the final. He'd been good company, and I liked him, but for once he could only get a few words out of me.

'Hard luck, bud,' he said, hand extended.

'Best of luck in the semi-final,' I replied as we shook.

The Kerry goalkeeper Brendan Kealy made his way towards me. He had one glove off, as did I.

I should really say thanks to him for the nice tweet he sent me after my article was published, I thought to myself. All I could muster was, 'All the best.'

I couldn't even look at the crowd as I exited the arena with my head hung low. I marched down the steps in the middle of the Cusack Stand and headed straight towards the dressing room in complete silence. The only noise I could hear was the sound of studs tapping on the hard, grey concrete floor. I pushed open the big yellow door and sat on my seat, which was the first on the left, as we were arranged in order of the number we wore out on the pitch. I leaned forward with my head in my hands and I felt the tears come straight away as I imagined life without football. Deep in the belly of Croke Park, just minutes after a crushing defeat, I sat there trying to make sense of what had just happened. I tried to gather my thoughts and feelings but realised that numbness and sadness were taking over.

I didn't have to worry about pulling a jersey off my sweaty back and over my head, as I had swapped it out on the field. The yellow Kerry goalkeeper jersey was in my hand and when I looked at it I couldn't help but wonder about what might have been if we had played like the real us in the first half. I placed the jersey over my face to hide the pain and the threatening tears from the rest of the group. I was like a child covering his own face in a game of hide-and-seek, or Father Dougal hiding behind that curtain in the caravan in *Father Ted*; I felt as if I could hide from everyone if I just couldn't see them.

I snapped back to reality and stuffed the jersey in my bag. Nobody asked me to throw my gear back into the middle of the dressing room like they had at every other battle I went into for Cavan in 2013. There was no need to prepare the armour for the next tussle.

Topless, I reached down to take off my black boots, the blue Cavan socks and white shorts, but I stopped when county board chairman Tom Reilly popped in to say a few words to the team. 'It's been a great year, but don't stop here. You have to come back stronger next year and keep fighting to improve Cavan football,' he said.

Terry Hyland spoke too. He had regrets, but said that as a group there was nothing we could do about the past, no matter how recent it was. As I sat listening to him, I prayed he wasn't stepping down, as in Cavan we knew better than most how hard it was to find good management teams. It was like a speech at a funeral; people were listening but they didn't really want to be there. It was horribly awkward, and I would have given anything to be elsewhere.

When they finally wrapped it up after what seemed like an eternity, our captain, Alan Clarke, stood up. He thanked everyone for their efforts and their support: the county board, the management, the physios, the masseurs, the players, the doctors and the kit men – all those who had given up their time for the betterment of the tribe over the past number of months. There was applause at the conclusion of each address but nothing like the energy-injecting ovation we had received when we'd run out onto the field earlier in the day, full of optimism.

Bodies slumped against the wall. I still had my shorts and socks on. I eyed them again and tried to summon the energy to remove them. I knew that when the last of my kit was off, the season was over after months of perseverance, resolve, commitment and effort.

I swallowed the lump in my throat and peeled off one sock, and then the other. I stood up to remove the last bit of my uniform, and took one last look around the room. I wanted to be able to remind myself of this devastating, demoralising low, so I could be sure to never feel like that again. It was a bit like taking the photo of the X-ray months earlier; I'd known I would need it in my memory to help inspire me at some time in the future.

I trudged to the showers to escape the horrible tension that had built up in the changing area. Some substitutes, including Conor Gilsenan, patted me on the back to express their consolation. I appreciated his kindness because I would have done the same for him. I pressed the button on the shower and let the hot water hit my face. I rubbed my hands up and down briskly on my skin but I couldn't wash the feeling away. The same feeling of hopelessness lingered no matter how hard I scrubbed.

I went to dry myself when I got back to my seat but it didn't seem like it was worth the effort. I wished there was a gadget nearby that would do it for me. Every rub of my arm or leg took its toll. I felt drained. I just wanted to lie down in a dark room by myself. I pulled on my Cavan tracksuit bottoms and T-shirt knowing it was the last time I would meaningfully wear them in 2013. The crest on the shirt seemed more prominent as I eyed it up. I studied it, noticing the red hand, the tower and the lake. It only reminded me how we had just let down our tribe and lost the war. I rammed my towel into my bag in frustration.

I noticed that my gear was now all over the place in my bag. I thought back to the bag I had prepared so neatly the previous evening in Bailieborough. I had even come back an hour after packing to take it all out and pack it again – just to be sure I was good to go. The boots were placed delicately on the left of the Cavan bag on top of a spare pair of similar boots. There were two pairs of identical black and orange Atak sports gloves on the opposite side, giving them plenty of space to avoid being crushed. The second pair on top had never even been worn, and I kept them with me in the goals in case the strapping on my hand burst the first pair at the seams. There were six cones in the bag too: two white, two blue and two orange – although I never liked kicking off anything other than blue and white cones when I was playing for Cavan.

Now everything was in a heap, thrown in every which way – a bit like my thoughts, a bit like my head. I closed it up and put the strap over my shoulder. I walked to the bus, lumbered miserably past some of the journalists I knew from working in the stadium and threw my bag in the hold. I was relieved no one asked to interview me.

I got on and found my usual seat a couple of rows back on the right – not too close to the management, but far enough away from the messing and joking that often took place at the back. Lads got on slowly and found their regular spots too, but this wasn't the same magical bus we'd arrived in. The atmosphere had soured; we were spent.

Some of the lads went straight to sleep, while others pretended to be in dreamland so they wouldn't have to engage in the charade of conversation. A few were staring into space with their earphones in, listening to music in an attempt to fight the grim mood that was pulling us all down, while some others tried to laugh and joke in an attempt to break the awkward silence and ease the tension.

Sequences from the game started to replay in my head. I visualised a kick-out that went a foot to the right of the hand where it should have landed; a tackle that one of the players missed as Colm Cooper worked a score; an attempted shot dropped short; a goal chance that blazed wide. I wondered how and why it had all gone wrong, and how the rollercoaster of it all could leave me in such a state so quickly. I was already dreading waking up the following morning and experiencing that all-too-familiar feeling.

There was about to be a huge void in my life, a drastic change to my weekly routine. I would soon have loads of time to myself, the one thing I wanted least in life. That scared me. Exiting the championship is an unpleasant experience for any player, but even at that early stage, I don't think it was the disappointment of the defeat itself that really got to me. It was like a part of me knew that the loss was going to give my depression a golden opportunity to pounce.

We had spent hundreds of nights and thousands of hours together trying to restore pride in our tribe: beating Monaghan and Meath in the league, that save against Sligo, breaking my arm, having to watch us beat Armagh and then cruelly lose to Monaghan before regrouping like a real winning team to overcome Derry in extra-time. I had got two outings in Croke Park as we reached an All-Ireland quarter-final, and we'd had both good times and bad in 2013. Together. I was proud of myself, and of all of us, but bitterly disappointed too that we hadn't advanced.

Back in Cavan, I watched the others filter out of the car park ahead of me. It was like soldiers leaving the army after finishing their service, peeling off in their own directions. They were signing off duty. The band of brothers, *my* band of brothers, was being dismantled. We had made so much progress and brought Cavan to latter stages of the All-Ireland series for the first time in 14 years. I was a much stronger and resilient character too.

As I slapped on the indicator and pulled out of the car park, I considered that maybe those people who had annoyed me over the years with their encouraging clichés after a bad loss were right. Maybe next year would be our year.

13
The Insomnia

Insomnia always reminded me of switching off the old computer we had in our house when I was a kid. As it prepared to make the screen go black, a pop-up box would appear saying: 'Windows is shutting down.' Whenever I was unable to sleep it always left me feeling trapped in that state. Unfortunately I couldn't unplug the power cord or remove the battery to force my brain into hibernation. So I had to lie there, staring at the ceiling in a world of my own.

Back in 2011, in the midst of an overpowering depression, the development of my insomnia had been a huge factor in my reaching out for help for the first time, even though I had yet to fully realise that I was depressed. When I had stopped sleeping I'd known I needed to consult my doctor, whereas with other symptoms, such as lack of energy or feeling down, I had convinced myself that I was just feeling sorry for myself.

Sleeping had been a sporadic problem since that spell in 2011, but I had figured out simple things that worked for me. I went out of my way to make sure I stayed in my own bed when possible so that I could maintain my usual routine, which helped. For a short spell, I chose not to stay overnight with my girlfriend following one particularly bad night in her bed watching TV shows on her laptop through headphones as she slept beside me peacefully. So I used to go over for the evening, kiss her goodnight and then head home around 11 p.m. I was disgusted at my depression for forcing me away from someone I cherished, but she completely understood and knew my sleeping problems were directly related to my ongoing struggle.

I rarely took the sleeping tablets I had been prescribed two years earlier by my local GP because I was afraid I would become dependent on them, but having the capsules to hand did ease the anxiety that insomnia caused. I hated nothing more than being stuck in that wakeful state all night, but I would never risk taking one the night before a game for fear that it would slow down my reflexes or decision-making the following day.

One night, a number of weeks after the Kerry defeat, I couldn't sleep, no matter what I did. I tried to remind myself that I was not alone in the insomniac club, that there were other people out there in the world feeling how I felt. I read a book, and tried to fall asleep to a relaxing playlist on Spotify that I'd named 'dreamy sleepy nighty snoozey snooze', but neither succeeded in helping me to wind down. As a last resort, I had a mindfulness CD that the founder of Headstrong, Tony Bates, had put together, which took me through several breathing exercises that encouraged my mind and body to shut off, but for the first time ever it didn't work.

As I grew more and more frustrated, my brain put forward a suicidal thought. Slowly, it made it seem like a logical way to stop the incessant chatter pulsing through my mind. I saw myself consuming every tablet I could get my hands on. However, the notion left my brain as quickly as it had come in. The whole process happened in seconds. In, out.

It was something I had grown used to over the previous few years – I had experienced countless suicidal thoughts by that stage. The difference was that through the work with Niall and the extraordinary learning curve I was climbing, I was now able to stop them translating into suicidal feelings. They rarely lingered anymore. They were a side effect of my depression that I had accepted, just like the headaches, the lack of energy and the itchy skin around my hands and scalp that the anxiety appeared to cause.

That acceptance was long in coming. In the early stages of my depression, the suicidal thoughts would cause absolute mayhem in my brain. I would weigh them up, consider what was causing them as I desperately tried to make sense of something I knew I should not be experiencing.

Rather than allow the irritation to consume me, I put my two hands behind my head and asked myself what was stopping me from switching off. What was I thinking about? Just what was it that was worrying me?

Come on, Alan, there is no point punching the pillow or feeling sorry for yourself. Let's try to make sense of this. Why am I not sleeping here?

I wondered if maybe I couldn't sleep because I had done little or no exercise in the previous few weeks. After pushing myself so hard for so long during the season, I wanted to take my foot off the gas and unwind for a little while. Plus, I had been told to rest a niggling injury in my right quad that had been troubling me during the summer in the hope that it would settle down. As it was important that I maximise the break in my schedule to aid the recovery, I hadn't played a game of football or trained for six weeks. Was it the release that playing sports provides me that I was missing? Or was I just not tired enough, having been used to so much strenuous exercise?

I couldn't help but wonder if maybe sport was not a release valve for me after all; maybe it was just a distraction. Did football just suppress all my feelings all year and was I now at a low ebb again because the Cavan season was over? I'd been similarly low when I'd been injured and not playing, so maybe it was true.

I typed everything that came into my head into

my phone. Even though I would rarely go back and read over what I had written, it always seemed to help slow my brain down when I was struggling with my mental health. It was like I could physically transfer the information from one hub to another.

A huge void was left in my life when Cavan exited the All-Ireland championship and it was something I struggled to cope with. I had had my struggles on and off throughout the year, but because of the crushing blow Kerry landed, the main thing that had injected drive, passion and motivation into my life throughout the year had disappeared. In the days and weeks that followed, I felt exhausted, and it was a feeling I struggled to shake off.

After my initial struggles with depression, I had put so much energy and effort into becoming the Cavan number one in 2013 that I'd felt that the achievement would be my salvation. It took over my life and it was all I cared about – especially after I broke up with my girlfriend. I used football as a distraction and focused on that instead of the other things that were happening in my life.

In a way, I think that by going public with my story, I put more pressure on myself to regain the Cavan jersey after my injury. I'm not saying I regret the decision to publish the article, because I don't, but part of me definitely felt that if I didn't regain my place at the top of the pecking order, my comeback year was a failure. I would just be the lad who had depression who couldn't even get a start for his county. I had chosen to focus attention on myself in order to raise awareness of depression and mental wellbeing. But with that, I felt that people's expectations of me on the field were higher than ever before, and that was not something I had considered in advance.

Either way, I got no downtime after the Kerry defeat to really digest it. The next weekend, I had been back in Croke Park for work, looking out on the same field and constantly wondering about my own performances. I also thought of how I'd felt during the second half of the Kerry game. I tried to live in the moment, to feel it like I did in 2011, but I had been numbed off again. It was weird how quickly depression could seize control of me.

Dublin's final tussle with Mayo had a lot of drama and action to get absorbed in as a spectator, but I felt almost nauseated by it. Like so many other supporters, part of me was jealous, and I wanted to be out there, of course I did, but the other part of me was resentful. I wasn't sure that I would ever again truly love the game of Gaelic football. I watched Bernard Brogan do what he does best and score 2-3, as Dublin became All-Ireland champions. I wondered if I would ever be able to play as freely as he did, it seemed to come so naturally to him. The former All-Star and Player of the Year looked so calm, confident and self-assured.

I wondered if I would ever be able to play right on the edge like that, with such admirable abandon. To me, that was the only way to really play football – the game had a special ability to take me to places that nothing else ever could. I worried that I was always going to feel mildly tortured whenever I stepped out in the Cavan jersey in the future.

By 3 a.m., I accepted that my body wasn't going to give in. I turned on the light beside my bed and hoped Netflix would help me to zone out. I figured it was better to embrace how my body felt rather than grow even more aggravated. I got lost in the world of *Criminal Minds*, fascinated by how agents Hotch, Reid, Prentiss and the rest of the team tried to understand the workings of others' brains. I was jealous of that ability – especially because I couldn't even make sense of my own.

I suddenly realised it was 6 a.m. and the alarm that I had set eight hours before was due to go off in an hour and a half. I wanted to talk to someone, anyone, but I couldn't. No one was awake – a search for Facebook friends confirmed that – and, tucked up in my bed, I felt completely and utterly alone. I thought about how everyone I knew was off in a happy dreamland at that exact moment – the little voice used it as a way to underline yet again how different I was. The theme ran that I just wasn't the same as everyone else because of my depression.

I pulled the pillow over my head and slapped my hand into it – contrary to what I'd promised myself earlier that night. I would have given anything at that moment for a single minute of inner peace. Out of nowhere, a yawn hit me and, at 6.11 a.m., I sensed my opportunity. I felt my body trying to switch off, but all of a sudden I started to worry about the following day. Would I be too tired at work? Should I call in sick? What mood was I going to be in after a night of no sleep? I reminded myself that worrying about the near future would do me no good. I heard Tony Bates's voice in my ear: 'Come back to the present moment.' A second yawn sealed the deal, and I finally got the serenity I craved.

When my alarm went off, I resisted the temptation to call in sick, lie in bed all day and feel sorry for myself. I dropped to the floor and did 20 press-ups. Then I let a hot shower jump-start my day. After getting dressed I headed to my car and drove to work in Croke Park.

I understood that when I struggled to sleep, something within me was off-balance. I tried to appreciate that I had a very clear warning signal – the onset of insomnia in 2011 had triggered my reaching out for help with regards to my mental health. Understanding what was happening and why I couldn't sleep was key to reducing the impact of the insomnia on my wellbeing. My insomnia was like those big flashing lights on the side of the motorway urging cars to slow down. I knew full well what my body was telling me, and I heeded the advice. Later that week, I booked an appointment with Niall.

I went back to the room and we began another process of reflection. It was through these sessions that it dawned on me just how unhealthy and toxic my relationship with football had become once more.

Yet I was so happy and willing to play throughout the year because it kept me in good company with like-minded people, and I enjoyed that. And the reality was, sure what else would I have been at? Out drinking and socialising every weekend like most other people that I knew? I didn't want that. I didn't want the predictable suffering that the hangovers brought. I also wanted a more meaningful life and to experience things that brought out my passion to succeed, things that gave me a strong sense of belonging. Up until then, I had failed to think of anything better than devoting my life to playing for Cavan.

'Niall,' I said, 'there's something wrong with me. I've been trying to work through this block, doing everything that normally works for me, but it won't leave. I can feel the depression hanging over me again. I just feel exhausted all the time. There is no respite from it at all.'

We went back over the season and the ups and downs since he'd last seen me when I'd had the cast on my arm.

'I'm glad I got back playing football, I really am, but in general it just wasn't the same. It wasn't like the magic of 2011. Don't get me wrong, it was good, but I had to put in so much more effort this time around. I was standing there in Croke Park in front of 60,000 people and it felt like a let-down somehow. I stood there on the biggest stage I have ever had the privilege to play on, looking around me in the second half thinking about how there had to be more to life than football, while legends like Declan O'Sullivan and Colm Cooper came at me. That's not right, is it? It was never like that before.'

He thought for a moment. 'Let me ask you something. What do you enjoy doing other than football, Alan?'

I sat in my chair gazing out the window. 'Mmm. Good question,' I replied. I failed to follow up with a sufficient answer.

'Come on, you have to have other things in your life that you enjoy doing?'

'Well, I went to the cinema the other night. I always enjoy that,' I said.

'So what's good about it?'

'My head goes quiet in the cinema. I get lost in the moment and, yeah, I like that. Who doesn't like Minstrels in popcorn as well!' I added with a chuckle. I was questioning everything and looking for answers, but I didn't have the same sense of hopelessness that depression used to bring.

'That's good. That's one good thing. What else have you got, then?'

'I'm struggling here, chief,' I said.

'I get you like going to the cinema, but I mean, do you ever really switch off?' He paused to hear what I had to say.

It clicked in my head straight away. My lifestyle

was both chaotic and robotic at the same time: chaotic in the sense that I was constantly busy with sporting commitments, while my emotions were forever fluctuating due to the nature of the game I devoted myself to and the pull it had on me. At the same time, all the structure meant that it felt robotic, pre-programmed, as I knew exactly what I was going to be doing nearly every week. I knew I was going to be on the rollercoaster each week, I just didn't know what way it was going to twist and turn. I realised I was getting none of what people tend to call 'me time'. I was just doing what I had to do to keep my depression at bay and get on the Cavan team. I was looking at life through a very narrow lens.

'Out of interest, when's the last time you went on a holiday, relaxed and got some sun on your back?' Niall asked.

'I don't know.'

'You don't know the last time you went on a holiday?'

'I can't remember exactly, like, it was a while back.'

'Well, what are we talking about here? A year? Two years? More?'

He was pressing for an answer, so I thought a bit harder. 'It was five years ago. I went to a wedding in Spain with herself for a few days,' I said. I went quiet for a second and thought about her. Was I depressed again because I didn't have her in my life? Was that where it was all coming from?

He sat back in his chair and looked at me. 'I wouldn't normally say this, but I recommend you get yourself a holiday. You've had a long year and it will do you good.'

When we worked through all of that out loud, it made so much sense to me. I was tired because I just hadn't stopped. I had invested so much in the last year to get myself in a position to run out in Croke Park on that sunny August day that nothing else had even got a look-in.

~

I was determined to take Niall's advice, and a few weeks later my little brother Billy and I booked an apartment in Lanzarote, jumping in on a week-long holiday my parents had planned. I had decided that the week would be about nothing other than relaxing and getting my energy levels back up. I had forgotten just how therapeutic I found being in a warmer climate.

I had gone on holiday to help myself feel better, and was all too aware of the risk that excessive drinking posed to my wellbeing. Consequently I had a few pints most days in a relaxed and enjoyable way to help me unwind and get into the holiday spirit, but nothing outlandish. It was exactly what I needed.

Midway through our getaway, the four of us were sitting around a table having a bite to eat. I had logged my phone out of all work-related accounts but kept myself signed in to my own social media. As I scrolled down the screen in the restaurant, one particular tweet caught my eye. I clicked on the link and started to read it.

My family were chatting away but I zoned out. My food arrived to the table but I had yet to give it any attention. I was engrossed in a piece of writing. I made it as far as the sixth paragraph before my eyes filled up with tears.

> Depression is difficult to explain to people. If you have experienced it there is no need; if you haven't, I don't think there are words adequate to describe its horror. I have had a lot of injuries playing hurling, snapped cruciates, broken bones in my hands 11 times, had my lips sliced in half and all my upper teeth blown out with a dirty pull but none of them come anywhere near the physical pain and mental torture of depression. It permeates every part of your being, from your head to your toes. It is never ending, waves and waves of utter despair and hopelessness and fear and darkness flood throughout your whole body. You crave peace but even sleep doesn't afford you that. It wrecks your dreams and turns your days into a living nightmare.

I had to stop reading. I had travelled thousands of miles in a desperate attempt to escape the feelings the author was describing and within a few seconds they all came flooding back to me. I could relate so much to what he was describing.

'What's that you're reading there?' asked my father, curious as to why I had gone so quiet all of a sudden.

'Ah nothing, just a piece about fantasy football,' I said, and put the phone down. I had to step outside for a moment to gather my thoughts.

Although I was yet to finish it, I knew already that this article by Conor Cusack meant a lot to me. He was a hurler, somebody who had played for Cork on the biggest stage there was, and he too was now opening up publicly and admitting to sinister feelings and the experience of depression. All those months ago, when I had published my piece, I'd been determined to start a conversation. In GAA circles anyway, one had now become two – the conversation had begun.

That break did go some way towards recharging my batteries, but I was still miles away from where I needed to be. However, I was about to share my story with a whole new audience, as I had been invited on to the *Saturday Night Show* hosted by Brendan O'Connor on RTÉ 1 television to discuss my experiences of mental health problems along with Niall Breslin, better known as Bressie. Both of us had become ambassadors for a wonderful organisation called Cycle Against Suicide, which promotes, in a fun and engaging way, the message that 'it is okay not to feel okay – and absolutely okay to ask for help'. The cycle visits a number of towns and schools over the course of a two-week tour around Ireland, hosting high-energy, entertaining events at each stop. I really enjoy working with the organisation and its founder Jim Breen to challenge the stigma of mental-health problems on our island.

Initially I was due to be a guest on the show at the beginning of August, but I couldn't deal with such a big distraction in the build-up to the Kerry game, so I'd cancelled. Then at a time when I was still feeling low and devoid of energy, I got dressed up, had my face covered in make-up and went on live national television to discuss what I had gone through almost two years previously. Very few knew how much of an ongoing battle it all was, though.

Bressie and I sat on the couch together as Brendan introduced us. There were dozens of lights shining on me from all different angles. I didn't know where to look or put my sweaty hands. I nervously fidgeted around in my seat as Brendan spoke to Niall. I remember nothing of what they said at the beginning, but Bressie looked so much calmer than me. It all went by in a haze.

Our discussion had been going on for 15 minutes or so and the only thing I remembered was worrying about whether the people at home could see my right leg shaking as it rested on top of my left knee. It all went by in a blur.

'How are you now?' asked Brendan as if he had just met an old friend at the supermarket picking up some milk from the fridge. Something changed in me and I completely relaxed.

When I looked back at the interview hours later, I could literally see how the composition of my face changed.

'I'm good. There can still be ups and downs. I suppose there are bad days and good days. I try to enjoy the good days a little bit more, and when there are bad days I try to remind myself that the good days are going to come back, and that it's okay not to feel okay,' I said.

Towards the end of that final sentence, there was a smile on my face and it summed up neatly how I had been surviving the previous few months. I gave away no details of my most recent troublesome spell – that was still my business as far as I was concerned.

Listening to Bressie speak towards the end of the interview made me understand that depression affects different people in different ways. I was being watched by hundreds of thousands of people on national television talking about mental health, but I was far from an expert. All I could talk about was my own experiences and what helped me get out of the spiral I was in. Niall, a former member of The Blizzards, a band whose music I'd played regularly in the mornings during my first year in college, talked about having panic attacks, something I had no real experience of despite my constant anxiety. It turned out we were both being kept awake at night by our depression, but in very different ways.

'You learn about it as you go through it,' said Niall. 'One thing I was always told by my family and friends was that I was very competitive. One of my mates said, "Why don't you approach your mental health like that? Why don't you get competitive with it?" What happened was, I would wake up at two in the morning and I would feel it coming – I'd feel my neck swelling and my chest getting tight. What I started doing then was I'd put on runners and I used to go out and run. I used to do this every time it came on and then after a few months it stopped coming. It started realising I was beating it. After two or three months of it, I never got another panic attack at night.

Brendan closed out the interview with a short conversation with Cycle Against Suicide founder Jim Breen, who was sitting in the front row of the audience. As he talked, I was able to sit back, relax and soak up the environment. I focused on my parents and my granddad Bill sitting directly beside Jim, as I had made a point of avoiding eye contact with them while I was speaking. I had a feeling that if my mother was close to crying during the interview, which she was, it would set off an emotional chain reaction with me. Sharing my story and my journey on that night with my parents looking on was one of my proudest moments.

My little brother Billy and I joined the Cycle Against Suicide crew for a few social drinks that night after my parents had left the green room to head home. My phone was hopping all night and my name was trending on Twitter. Sometimes when I did media interviews I wondered if the hype was actually helping people. I preferred to talk directly to young people in classrooms or lecture theatres, or to people face to face, but that night really drove home the importance of sharing real stories and having meaningful conversations about mental health in front of a large audience. People were congratulating me for speaking so openly and honestly about such a sensitive topic – telling me how brave I was and how much hope I had given them.

It was nice to get all that positive feedback – of course it was – but what I really took home from that night was a better understanding of how people experience depression in so many different ways. Just as he had given the nation pause for thought, Niall Breslin had made me see my own situation in a new light. Even though we were fighting the same beast, his interview made clear that we had very different ways of dealing with our low points. I understood that although I had built up ways to survive and keep on top of my depression, I wasn't getting beyond it. I wanted more. I wanted to thrive.

I was constantly battling with it, fighting it off and competing for control, and I wasn't happy to settle for that any longer. As my head hit the pillow that night, I knew that I would have to make significant changes in my life.

14

The Changes

I didn't understand why I wasn't feeling fulfilled, so I embarked on a pursuit of happiness and made some significant changes in my life.

First I decided to transfer from my home team in Bailieborough and join St Oliver Plunkett's/Eoghan Ruadh GAA club in Dublin towards the end of 2013. I was trying to set up a home and a life where I was working and paying rent, yet almost every spare second I had seemed to be spent in Cavan because of my commitment to football. A lot of young people from rural Ireland have that relationship with their home town during their college days, but as I was getting older and now working full time, I wanted to lay down roots. If I could really commit to where I was living, I'd be better placed to meet new people and develop new support networks. With the nature of my work, I knew I was going to be living in Dublin for the foreseeable future, so it seemed like a sensible move. It was an important step towards being more independent, and deciding what I wanted to do with my time without feeling like I had to run home every weekend to play football.

Things had been most problematic at weekends. After training on Friday in Kingspan Breffni Park I would just sit in the house, waiting to go to football on either the Saturday or the Sunday. I had no real social life while I was there, because none of the friends I had grown up with still lived in our home town anymore – they were all in Dublin, London or even farther afield. So I was sitting in work all week thinking about GAA, and then sitting in my parents' house at the weekend doing the same. The balance seemed completely wrong to me, and declaring for a team in Dublin seemed like a logical solution.

Transferring the way I did is very controversial in GAA circles, as the tradition would be 'one life, one club' – the whole fabric of the association is built on the principle of people supporting their local club and their county. As an employee of the GAA, I absolutely respected those values, but the reality is that transfers into the capital are now more common than ever, for the simple reason that Dublin is where most of the jobs are. Some players can manage the sacrifices inherent in the inevitable travel, juggling the demands of work, sport and personal life in order to play for their home team, but the burden of those commitments just wasn't right for me anymore.

I had reached a point where I simply wanted to prioritise my own wellbeing and enjoyment of the game over what other people thought of me and traditions that had been developed when Ireland was a very different place. Transferring had been in my mind for some time and it got to the point where it seemed such a logical and simple solution that I could no longer ignore it.

The Bailieborough Shamrocks lads were very accepting and understanding of my move when I had explained my reasoning. It helped that Conor Gilsenan, two years my junior, lived on their doorstep and was a ready-made replacement for me on a senior team I'd first played for when I was 16.

I made my debut for Oliver Plunkett's in a frantic league game against St Vincent's and was blown away by the speed and quality of the match. It was open, attacking football like I had never seen before. Around 15 minutes into the game, I was completely baffled by the amount of space that was left in front of my goals for the opposition to exploit. I had come from a Cavan team that had implemented one of the strongest defensive units of the All-Ireland championship.

During a break in play, I strolled out to my corner-back Michael Brides, a former Cavan player himself who had moved to the club from Redhills a number of years before me. 'Is it always like this, Bridesy?' I asked, pointing to the space in front of us. Mossy Quinn, a former Dublin forward, had already poked two goals past me.

'Yep,' he said, before he had to go running after his man, who had the run of the park.

'Fuck me. This is mental,' I said aloud.

The next night at training, the players had a meeting to seek a change of management. A change had been planned for the end of the season, but I didn't expect it to come so soon. Gareth 'Nesty' Smith, who had also spent some time on the Cavan panel, had been a strong factor in my joining the club. He had left me in no doubt as to the potential of the group, which featured two former Players of the Year in brothers Alan and Bernard Brogan, and I also knew Conor Walsh from my time in DIT. I sat in complete silence throughout the meeting. I caught Nesty's eye and raised an eyebrow that said, 'You have sold me a dud, Del Boy.'

My groin problems forced me to miss our last few league games but I tried to stay involved with the panel as much as I could, and I regularly went to watch training and games. I was fully determined to integrate into the group and build up a new support network around me.

When the 2014 season came around under the new management team of Pat McDonagh and Paul Clarke, I was also back training with Cavan and that meant I didn't spend anywhere near enough time with my new teammates because they trained on the same nights as my county team. I felt a bit like a random outsider who just turned up to play games when I was released from Cavan duty, but that's how it went: the two seasons run at the same time, so you are constantly trying to balance commitments to both teams.

Despite my building depression, I started the first round of the Dublin club championship against Kilmacud Crokes in May. It was a seriously high-quality affair that surpassed anything I had ever experienced while playing at club level in my home county. I was playing with the Brogans, Ross McConnell and Declan Lally, all of whom had featured with Dublin for years, as well as Shane Lyons, who was an excellent player for Fermanagh.

Crokes, boasting Dublin players of their own such as Rory O'Carroll, Paul Mannion and Cian O'Sullivan, were an extremely formidable outfit, but we recovered from conceding an early goal to emerge victorious. It was even sweeter for me as I saved a penalty from Mannion in the latter stages of the second half when they were trying to get back into the game. Again, I was surprised by how capable I was of pulling a good performance out of the bag when my head was not in a great place.

The post-match celebrations would have been a good time to get to know my teammates even better, but as most of the lads went out that night, I had to travel to Gormanston in County Meath to join up with the two-day Cavan training camp ahead of the start of the Ulster championship.

As well as that huge change in my life, I had also made the decision to leave my post in Croke Park in search of a new professional challenge. I had grown weary of the 'always-on' world of social media and I felt the GAA was dominating too much of my life, given how I both worked for the organisation and gave so much of my time to playing its games.

In the aftermath of going public with my story, I had been inundated with requests to speak at public functions and schools in relation to positive mental health. After overcoming my nerves about sharing my story in front of a group, it was something I had really settled into and enjoyed doing. It brought me a sense of satisfaction, one that my role in the GAA could never match.

The day after I had started for Cavan in our McKenna Cup final defeat to Tyrone in February, I gave a talk to students of St Ciaran's in Ballygawley. It was a school with a strong GAA pedigree, and I had actually played against them many years earlier. I felt an extremely strong connection with the students during my presentation. They listened thoughtfully and were really lively and engaged when the time came to ask questions. I left that school in no doubt that I had made a positive contribution.

My phone rang later that week. 'A letter is here for you, Alan. Do you want me to open it?' asked my mother.

'Yeah, belt away. What is it?' I asked.

'Oh my God, you have to see this. I can't explain it,' she said. I could sense the shock in her voice.

A teacher in the school had taken the time to

ask her students to each write down on a piece of paper what they had liked about my talk and the key ideas they took away from it. When I sat down a couple of days later to read through them, my eyes welled up with tears. I couldn't believe how willing those students had been to open up in their short notes, and to speak so honestly and intelligently at such a young age. They were so grateful to hear my experiences, and what really struck me was how different students related to the talk in different ways. For some it struck a chord in their own life, while others thought of siblings or parents and how they could be more supportive to them in the future.

Describing such a personal and emotional journey can be incredibly draining, and sometimes I wondered afterwards just how much the reliving of my own experience was actually helping others. I also questioned whether it was good for me to be constantly bringing up so much of my past.

Without knowing it, that teacher and her students ensured I would never have to worry about answering those questions again. I've kept those notes, and if I ever question the importance of being a mental-health advocate or lack energy or motivation before I go to deliver a talk, I sit down and reread them. It may sound extreme, but I realised that I had the ability to help save lives. That was a powerful feeling to have.

I was able to discuss all this with Fran O'Reilly of Amaze, an organisation that specialises in helping people to develop their potential and challenging those who feel they are capable of more. He quickly became an inspiring mentor to me. This guidance was funded by the Gaelic Players Association, who were once again an incredible support, and their interest in my personal life and development is something for which I will be forever grateful. The GPA had helped save my life with the counselling service, and then did all they could to improve it through the personal development programme.

Fran is an amazing man who prides himself on helping people find their calling. He is wise and caring, an illuminating beacon who helped me find my way and understand what the right working environment was for me. He believes in the theory of a 'primed mind', which is based around the principle that thoughts become things. We had been talking regularly about what I would like to do for a living, and I wasn't convinced that there was a job out there that would allow me to make a meaningful difference. Until one day a link appeared on my Twitter feed, which I duly opened.

The job description was almost a carbon copy of the wish list Fran and I had put together over the course of several meetings. I couldn't believe it. I applied and was invited to interview. I sneaked out of Croke Park to attend the meeting, and a couple of hours later Ian Power, the director of SpunOut.ie, called to offer me the role of Communications and Fundraising Officer.

I was thrilled. I was going to be working for a youth information website that supplied helpful and non-judgemental information to young people on vital matters like mental health, physical health, education and employment.

The changes had been made. Onwards and upwards, I thought.

~

Niall took a deep breath and looked at me.

'Look,' he said, 'I have hinted at this before, but I have never felt you were ready to take it on board before now. When did we first see each other?'

'Back at the start of 2012,' I confirmed.

'Well, at the start, the work we did was enough to get you back living your life and back out into the world. We talked about a lot, and you reflected on a lot, but I think we both knew there was always another level that you needed to dig down into and work through. I think that time has arrived.'

'What do you mean?' I wondered. It all sounded a bit airy-fairy.

'Just in terms of accepting yourself and really reflecting on who you are as a person, what you enjoy and being true to yourself.'

'I'm not really following here, Niall.'

'Okay, try this. Describe yourself to me. Who are you?'

'I'm Alan O'Mara.'

'That's your name, but who are you? What makes

you, well, you?' said the man who had helped me work through so much.

'I suppose people will always say, "There's the Cavan keeper. He's happy and outgoing."' I wasn't sure if that was the right answer.

'That's not what I mean. That's what other people see. Let's try this a different way, because you are a writer – you're good with words. Give me a couple of words that best describe you as a person.'

'Eh . . . intelligent?' I said, before waiting to see if I was on the right track.

He nodded in approval.

'Eh . . . thoughtful?' I added.

'Thoughtful in what way?'

'I suppose I just get on well with people. A lot of times, if people are going through something, they tend to come to me for a chat or ask for advice. I don't go looking for it, they just tend to find me.'

'That's good. You're on the right track. Between now and our next visit, I want you to take some time to think about what makes you you. Who is the real Alan O'Mara? Not the one people see playing in Croke Park, not the one people see in a pub or a nightclub, in the dressing room or at work. I want you to really think about who you are and what you enjoy doing, regardless of what other people think.'

'Eh . . . okay,' I said. Part of me hadn't a clue what he was talking about, but he had piqued my interest. This was new ground. We weren't just talking about my past, or reactions and feelings to certain events.

'You don't sound convinced,' said Niall.

'I just . . . I mean . . . I don't know where to start with all this. I've never thought about myself in this way before,' I replied.

'Trust me. Keep a list of what words you think best define you. Make a list of the things you do or that happen to you that allow you to feel most like you. Try new things. Try going to the theatre, to a comedy gig or a festival, and don't be afraid to challenge your friends to try new things with you. Break the habits that you're not happy with and get out of what you think is your comfort zone.'

Habits. I thought about that word a lot when I got home that evening. For most, life is just one long line of habits really. I drove to work the same way every morning, even though there were three or four routes that all took the same time. For some reason, I drove home an entirely different way. Why? Because it was a habit!

I began to question everything I did and why I did it. As habits went, few things puzzled me as much as my relationship with alcohol. There was no denying I had used it to escape more than I should have during my college years, but it wasn't always like that. I'd had my first real drink at 16 years of age, when I was in my final year in school and getting ready for my Leaving Cert. Some of the students had organised a 'Pre-Debs', which was basically an excuse to get dressed up, drunk and forget about exam stresses.

All my friends were going but my father was

adamant that I wasn't, given that I wasn't of age. At 16, I was the youngest person in my year by a good bit, and while others had started to hit the town regularly on a Saturday night, I had yet to join them. It didn't bother me at all, because I was on my first year with the county minor panel and we had training most Sunday mornings. However, this was one time I felt I needed to bow to the peer pressure and attend. In the end, Dad allowed me to go, but told me he was collecting me at 1 a.m. I reluctantly said an early goodbye to my friends, came out to the car on time and in good shape, and pretended as best I could to be fully sober.

Over the years, my reluctance to consume alcohol had diminished, and I'd enjoyed going out as much as anyone else. I'd probably enjoyed the new-found freedom in college a little bit too much, but that was all part of growing up and finding my feet in the world. I had worked in a pressurised job in the *Cavan Post* for a year, and felt I deserved more than most to enjoy that way of life.

That had all changed by the time I was in the fourth year of my degree, when depression was wreaking havoc. When I look back now, I really don't like the person I was during that spell – particularly when I hit the beer. At no point was I an alcoholic, but I did consistently choose to get drunk as a way to escape my own thoughts and feelings.

I'd been my worst following the break-up with my girlfriend and I'd taken an extremely cavalier approach towards women while I was under the influence of alcohol. I had been in a loving relationship for a long time and that was really all I knew. The single game and hunting for the shift had been new to me. I'd lost a sense of my own identity by constantly going out on the beer. To hide the pain of my heartache, I'd put on a mask and pretended I was revelling in my freedom. The problem was, I'd forgotten it was just a disguise and kept it on for far too long.

Usually I'd drink eight cans of the cheapest beer and a naggin of vodka before I even reached the nightclub, so when I woke the next day in a house full of lads with a hangover and depression aggravated by alcohol, my night often felt like a failure if I hadn't pulled. It was shallow and meaningless, but in a way I'd felt it was what I'd had to do in order to truly enjoy the college experience. I felt the pressure to conform and caved in to it. In my search for a new identity, I'd turned into that stereotypical jock often seen in American movies. Deep down, however, I was anything but.

Getting drunk and having fun with women was my way of coping with the heartbreak caused by the end of my loving relationship – it was a pain that had taken me a long time to fully digest. I'd wandered around like a drunken fool on nights out, not sure if I wanted to find love again with someone new, if I wanted to avoid giving any commitment at all to women or if I was still in love with my ex.

The chances of filling the void with a new loving

relationship were slim, given that I was rarely the loving, caring and respectful person I had been. Incapable of deciding what I wanted, I'd refused to show the women I pursued or slept with any real affection. The break-up had damaged me far more than I realised at the time.

I stuck to friends-with-benefits relationships, and when I look back now, the women I saw must have thought I was so cold and heartless. I would point-blank refuse to show any affection even after sex, and would often leave after we had finished fooling around – I'd known I wouldn't be able to sleep in a strange bed because of my insomnia and restless mind. I certainly had no intention of sitting on the end of the bed and telling a woman I had depression, insomnia and all that jazz. It was easier just to leave and hope she wouldn't tell all her friends.

Through counselling, I'd learned a lot about my relationship with alcohol, as well as women, and it changed my life for the better. I also didn't want sex to replace alcohol as my preferred method of escapism. I was very reluctant to ever fall back on either again, so for a period I avoided nights out with people my own age in favour of relaxed evenings with work colleagues with quiet pints and opportunities for proper chats. Some people had looked at me like I had seven heads when I started being truer to myself and admitting that nightclubs weren't really my scene, but it was worth it. I had been trying to challenge the ideas and expectations

I had for myself, concepts of what a man should be that had developed at a very confused time in my life. I recognised that being honest about what I wanted and how I felt didn't make me any less of a man.

To really kick-start the rebuilding process, I decided that I had to focus on the list I'd discussed with Niall, because I felt that I was very different to the noncommittal and cocky version of myself I'd been recently. It was time to recognise my true attributes and learn how to let them shine.

That was the real thing that had to change.

15
The Call

I was sitting in my black Volkswagen Golf on a warm day in early May, directly outside Niall's office in Dublin, and it had finally dawned on me that I could not go on as I had been. My lifestyle was no longer sustainable.

I had competed with my depression for so long but it had reached a tipping point. I was working hard with Niall to process the emotional baggage within me but football kept getting in the way of that process. I regularly put commitments to training and the team ahead of my mental health priorities and that had to change to allow to me truly feel the benefit of the most recent spell of counselling.

It was time to take another step back from the game I loved in order to reflect on my life. I had switched GAA clubs and changed jobs. I had also moved in to a house in Dublin with my brother Billy at the beginning of 2014 – as an opportunity had come up to move into the house of a relation who had emigrated to China – but I still wasn't happy. Clearly, what was happening inside me was causing the problems and not my circumstances.

Having just started a new job with SpunOut.ie, I had to call in sick early on as the depth of my illness ensured that I simply could not function at anywhere near a professional standard. The main problem was that my depression came with shocking headaches that sat right at the front of my head between my eyebrows and my hairline. They were deep, dull and unforgiving, and no painkiller ever helped to ease them. Despite all I had learned, I lay in bed for days on end, angry and resentful that I had been hindered in my progress so drastically once more.

One of the major things that helped me during that joyless spell was that rather than lying to those around me, I was able to tell them the truth.

As an organisation that focused on young people's wellbeing, SpunOut.ie practised what it preached, and the understanding I got from the team of Niamh, John, Tricia, Cian and Ian during an incredibly difficult time was immeasurable. I wish every work environment in Ireland could be as open and sensitive as that one, and I am privileged to call them friends. I often found the conversations around my mental health awkward at first, but the continued support I received from family, friends, new work colleagues and the GAA club was extremely comforting.

The despairing voice in my head, as prominent as it

had been for so long, tried to tell me that I was going to lose my job because of my ineptitude – but it was wrong. I was eased back into work gradually after a short break, and the job stuck. Part of my remit was to be the public voice of SpunOut.ie in the media, but my boss Ian temporarily took over some of that to alleviate the pressure on me. He told me to focus on the less stressful parts of the role until I felt ready.

As I had changed so much in my life in the search for happiness, the moment had come to embrace my past and who I really was as a person, and I had to look deep within for answers. It simply wasn't acceptable to let external forces, such as a football career, work or a relationship, consume my identity any longer. I wanted a fulfilling life instead of simply existing. I had to take control, and rather than slotting into different environments and making myself fit in it was time to stick to the list I had drawn up with Niall and grow into an authentic version of myself.

I swallowed, gripped the handbrake and held the phone up to my ear. I stared at the shiny silver button at the top of the brake shaft and it was the perfect metaphor for me. With our 2014 Ulster championship campaign just around the corner, I needed to press eject.

I waited anxiously for the ringing tone to stop. 'Terry, Alan here. How's the form?'

'Ah, I'm not too bad, I suppose. More importantly, how are you?' he asked, upbeat.

Not for the first time, silence lingered between us

on the phone as my brain worked rapidly to construct a sufficient response. The truth was, I was absolutely terrible. I had just walked out of a counselling session, and it had been deeply hurtful to lay bare how rotten and incredibly low I was feeling. I had been struggling to gather an ounce of positivity in any area of my life for as long as I could remember, despite the changes I had made.

Through my new job, I knew I wanted to help young people get information that could help them navigate the life challenges they faced, but I was struggling to find the motivation to perform – or even to get out of bed in the morning. The move to Oliver Plunkett's had certainly reduced the burden of travel, but it hadn't yet reignited my love for the game in the way I had hoped. When the Cavan season had recommenced at the beginning of 2014, I was back where I started: spending my weekends twiddling my thumbs in Bailieborough and waiting to go to football.

One night after the conclusion of our league campaign, while I was sitting on the couch and not in the best of form, my dad looked over at me. 'Alan, what are you at?'

'What do you mean?' I asked.

'Like, what are you doing here?' he said.

'I've football tomorrow, sure.'

'I know that, but you just come home here every weekend and sit around until you have to go to a match or training. You're just not . . . living your life. I mean, most weekends you spend sitting in with me and your mam.'

I was a bit taken aback; those words really drove a message home to me, and the conversation remained etched in my memory. I knew that my parents, being from Dublin, never fully understood my passion for Cavan football to begin with, but the fact that they, like me, were questioning the knock-on effect the game was having on my life made a big impression. That honest assessment from my father moved me another step closer to removing inter-county football from my life. I heard his voice in the back of my head as I began the conversation with Terry.

'To be honest, Terry, I'm not good. I'm not good at all. My head is gone. I've tried everything that normally works and I just can't get this block of depression to pass. Right now, it is as bad as it was the first time, if not worse.'

It felt worse because, this time around, I knew exactly what was going on: I knew it was depression. I remembered everything I had learned in counselling, and I knew I was more self-aware than ever before, but none of it was making me feel any better.

'Is there anything we can do for you? Would you like a break from training, or is the training helping? I know you said to me before how the training tends to be a good thing for the head when you are having tough patches,' he said.

'Well, that's just it, Terry. For some reason, it just

doesn't seem to be making me any better anymore. In fact, I think it's actually making me worse.'

'How do you mean?' he asked, the curiosity rising in his voice.

'I don't know, but I am just not enjoying my football at the minute. I haven't been enjoying it for some time. I just feel like I am in a negative frame of mind all the time and I think I am bringing negative vibes into the dressing room. It's at the stage where I almost feel guilty for being in there with the lads. I think you would be better off without me.'

'Well, I haven't noticed that, and I'll be honest with you, it hasn't transferred across into your training or performances. We were only talking the other night about how well you were moving the past few weeks,' said Terry.

I got a flashback to a save I made from Mickey Lyng in training. He had dummied me and left me flat on my backside, but by the time he'd stepped around me I was back on my feet and clawed that ball out of his hands with my outstretched right paw. He stood there in disbelief for about five seconds trying to understand how I had denied him the goal. I heard one of the lads behind the goals say, 'That is some fucking save, O'Mara.' Even this failed to reignite the fire in my belly.

'Well, I just don't feel that, Terry. Football is meant to be a hobby, I'm meant to love doing it, but I'm getting into the car giving out about having to go to training and I just feel like I'm going through the motions. I think I need to step off the panel for a while.'

'Can I ask, is the fact you haven't been playing driving this?'

I paused for a second to gather my thoughts. I missed the entire pre-season due to the ongoing niggles in my groin and hip region and, as it transpired, I gave Conor Gilsenan too big of a head start in the race to get in between the posts. He slotted into the goals for the first league game and stayed there as we went on an unbeaten run of seven matches to secure promotion. As hard as I tried, I couldn't catch him as the goalkeeper very rarely gets changed when the team is winning. Maybe Terry was on to something. Maybe if I played, I'd feel better.

Despite my lack of match practise and training, Terry had started me in the McKenna Cup final against Tyrone on 19 February – the original final had been delayed due to adverse weather conditions. I had made two really good saves to deny them certain goals, but I'd never felt comfortable. I'd been rusty, anxious, lacked sharpness and was very nervy. The doubts were there and I was second-guessing myself again. I knew I had failed to put my best foot forward.

When the National League began soon after, Conor had been given the nod to start. Our defensive system performed exceptionally well in the first six games and the opposition managed just one solitary shot on target between them, which Conor smartly saved. He hadn't put a single foot wrong throughout the campaign.

As the year had progressed, my depression had risen in tandem with the desire to become the number one again – just like I was in 2013. Changing clubs, jobs and moving house had done little to alleviate it because the fact remained that I hadn't yet come to accept who I was as a person. I was still looking for things like football to provide my self-worth and sense of purpose, so I still felt that if I could get back out on the pitch, my mental struggles would ease. Again, it was terrible rationale and made my relationship with the game even more toxic.

After game five against Longford, with a 100 per cent record intact, our promotion to the second tier had been secured and I had expected to be given an opportunity – but I was disappointed. Terry chose to leave me on the bench against Roscommon in the next fixture. I was livid and I felt let down. My mind was in a fragile enough state and all I could think about was how he must not trust me anymore. He had no idea how much I needed it, because I kept it all to myself. I'd cornered him after training to vent how I was feeling and demanded clarification.

'We decided to change a few of the lads around out the field and we didn't want to mess with the spine of the team too much, because we want to make sure we keep momentum going. You will be starting the next day,' he'd told me in the tunnel of Kingspan Breffni Park, calmly leaning up against the door that led out onto the main field. I'd told him how disappointed I was and how I'd genuinely believed that I deserved to start the Roscommon game, but his mind had been made up and my pleas had fallen on deaf ears.

Regardless of my feelings that night, Terry was true to his word, and I kept a clean sheet against Limerick in our final league game. We had won all seven games in a division where we had flirted with relegation for years under Tommy Carr and Val Andrews – it was a considerable achievement and added to the feeling that Cavan was very much a team on the rise.

I'd played well, and felt much more composed than in the final defeat to Mickey Harte's men. My kick-outs were excellent and, in particular, I'd struck up a good relationship with Philip Tinnelly, who was playing at right wing-back and also getting his first real run-out of the year. My good performance had done little to alleviate the depression that had been weighing me down and only then had I started to genuinely consider that my life would be better without football. It clearly just wasn't going to be the answer at this juncture.

'Look, obviously the fact I've been a sub for most of the league hasn't helped, but this is something bigger than simply playing or not playing. You know I hate being a sub, but it's now at the stage where I can barely get out of bed in the morning. I've missed days off work in my new job because I am so depressed.'

'I'll be straight with you, Terry, I'm sitting outside my counsellor's place right now where we've just spent the last hour discussing whether I should leave the panel. It's not something I have just decided on a whim or in the heat of the moment. You know me well, and you know how much I love playing for Cavan, but I really think this is something I need to do for me.'

'My head is all over the place at the minute and I really need to focus on that. It's impossible for me to enjoy my football when I am like this. I just feel like I can't give myself the time, energy or focus to get to the bottom of this when I am trying to push myself to play for Cavan.'

'Okay,' he said, hesitating. It was clear he wasn't expecting to have this conversation when he answered the phone. He probably thought I was going to be pestering him about my chances of starting in the team, but he had no idea how far that had dropped down my list of priorities. 'Look, there is no need to make any big decisions now. We have a big game coming up against Armagh, and if all goes well then I would hate for you to miss out on something down the line. Just do me one favour, will you? Take some time to think all this over and we'll touch base again in a few days, all right?'

'No, Terry, I really just need to do this. You know what I am like when my mind is made up, and as much as I don't want to do it, this is the right thing for me. I need to feel like the decision has been made in my head. I need some sort of clarity,' I said, a bit more forcefully than was my usual manner.

'I want you on the panel, I want you to know that. We both know you have struggled with injuries and form all year, there's not much that can be done about that, but I certainly don't want you to go and I know the lads won't either.'

The two voices in my head were screaming at me. I was in a complete state of flux. It felt like the biggest decision I had ever made in my life. I knew it had to happen, but the reality was that stepping away from the panel terrified me. So much of my identity and my life had been defined by putting on that jersey over the years.

My comfort zone and my weekly schedule were being destroyed. I was choosing to change. I was stepping out of the shadow that was overpowering my life and going at it alone. It was time to focus on me. I had to discover more about Alan O'Mara than what the Breffni colours could tell me.

'I appreciate that. I really do, but even my counsellor has suggested some time away from the game could help me at the moment. It just can't go on like this. I've just started a new job and whatever spare energy I have for now needs to go towards that,' I said.

'Okay, Alan. I can see your mind is made up. Look it, as long as I am the manager of this team, the door will be open for you. I mean that. Pick up the phone to me anytime. Let's stay in touch regardless of whether you come back or not in the next few weeks. I hope you feel better soon. Keep going, you have been through it before, and you will get there again,' he added.

It was an honest, sincere and caring remark that has long stuck with me. I probably would have bowed if the conversation with Niall immediately beforehand hadn't made the matter so clear in my mind. We had spoken at great length just before I called Terry because I was scared that I would be haunted by my decision if Cavan went on to win an Ulster title. As well as that, it was even harder to walk out on the man who had helped me win my first provincial crown over three years earlier.

'Thanks, Terry, chat soon,' I replied, and hung up.

I was liberated. I was devastated. I was happy. I was sad.

What had I done? Every emotion possible churned around my body as I sat in the car. I was still parked on Niall's road, but I felt like I was moving at the speed of light. My chest tightened. My eyes filled with tears. There was anger, and then guilt. Regret, and then hope.

I had given so much to play for Cavan in 2013 and then chose to give up on the team. I wanted that Ulster medal; I wanted that prestige – but just not as much as I wanted to be a happy person again.

My depression was so deep. It had sucked the happiness out of me like the world's most powerful hoover. Yet in a way I was almost glad it was there because it had made me recognise and appreciate how important my wellbeing really was, more important than my sporting career. I wasn't looking to the thousands of people in the crowd to help me feel good about myself anymore. I was only looking towards one place for that, and that was deep within me.

'Tell me why you are quitting, Alan. Why walk away now?' Niall had asked an hour earlier in the room.

'It's like this: over the past few years, I've learned a lot from working with you, and one of those things was the fact that I need to have several strong pillars in my life. One of those is my family, another is my friends, and football has always been there – I accept that and it has helped me a lot over the past few years. I have work too, and recently I've added the charity stuff that I do in my own time that I know is helping other young people. I've built up a decent spread of supports, so that if one comes crashing down for whatever reason, the others can pick up the slack and keep me going.'

'But you see, here's the problem I have at the minute. I think my life has those four or five pillars, and don't get me wrong, I am grateful to have them. But the reality is that football is not a pillar anymore. It is a 60-foot skyscraper soaring way above everything else. It overpowers everything and I really feel I need to redress that balance. How am I meant to work through this, to think about my depression and reflect on other things, when basically I am running around like a headless chicken trying to get playing for my county?

'This depression hasn't really left me since I came to see you again in October of last year. It's not fair and I am sick of it. I am exhausted. You know I pride myself on not giving in, but I can't do it anymore. I just can't.'

'That's a pretty strong argument. It sounds like your mind is made up, then,' Niall had said.

I had slowly raised my chin towards the ceiling and back down again. Something my older brother David had said days earlier stuck with me. 'When the ship is sinking, you offload the heaviest things first to try to keep it afloat.' We had both nodded in agreement.

There was no doubt that my biggest burden was football. It needed to be cut loose for the sake of the others.

Niall had brought my focus back to the room. 'Okay then, take a break and give yourself some time. And remember, you are not retiring from playing inter-county football here and now, so don't think you are making a permanent decision. You are just stepping away, and many lads have done it before for so many different reasons and they will do so again. Your health is far more important right now and I think you need to focus on that and address it before you worry about football again.'

It was time to find the real me.

It all felt so wrong. Yet it also felt so right.

16
The Mask

My decision to withdraw from the Cavan panel wasn't the first step I'd taken to change things, but it stood to liberate me – my time, my mind, my body – in a more stark way than anything I'd done so far. But it took more than a phone call to feel its positive effects.

After leaving the topsy-turvy world of inter-county football in 2014, I had prioritised achieving a clear understanding of my emotional wellbeing. I had contacted the Plunkett's management team of Pat McDonagh and Paul Clarke to tell them that I needed a short break, and thankfully they had also told me to come back whenever I felt myself again. Their empathy and compassion meant a lot, because for years my brain had told me that I could not show any vulnerability or weakness in the testosterone-driven environment of a male GAA dressing room. Being transparent about my situation hadn't diluted or destroyed my relationships like the voice had wanted me to believe it would; it had strengthened them.

Later in the year, four months after I had left the Cavan panel, I had enjoyed a superb run with St Oliver Plunkett's/Eoghan Ruadh that had ended with a one-point defeat to the reigning All-Ireland champions St Vincent's in the final of the Dublin senior football championship in Parnell Park. It was a disappointing loss but it had reminded me that one day I would be able to have a positive relationship with the game again. I had played through an ankle injury that required surgery in the off-season, but even though I had those limitations and knew I was not playing at my best, I had sensed an old love for the game bubbling somewhere deep beneath the surface.

Despite conceding just one goal in four championship games and being nominated for a 'Dubs Star', the Dublin club equivalent of an All-Star, I had stuck with my decision and didn't go back to the Cavan squad in 2015. I really felt I was making significant progress through the latest body of work and it was something I wanted to continue to focus on. I worried that running back to play for Cavan would hinder that progress.

During the previous months, Niall and I had dug deep into my depression and identity. I had finally fully accepted that for too long I had been looking for happiness from external sources rather than from within. I was feeling unstable because I had purposefully chosen to leave my comfort zone and had made so many changes, but they had failed to turn my life around the way I had planned.

In search of the answers, I travelled back to my past with Niall's help. We ventured deep into the archives of my mind. I wanted to focus on who I was as a person before football had taken over my life.

I was a quiet, unassuming child for the first 12 years of my life in Donaghmede in Dublin. The thing I had enjoyed most was reading books and getting lost in fictional worlds that seemed so much more exciting than where I lived. I had loved my own company and spent hours exploring my own imagination. I didn't think there was anything odd about that and reading was one of my favourite hobbies.

I had done well in school and at sports and I felt fairly confident about myself. Back then, I was willing to stand up and fight for Alan O'Mara if I had to, and one boy, who had fancied himself as a boxer, took a dislike to me. I had never been in a proper fight in my life, but one day during lunch in my primary school I had seen him out of the corner of my eye coming towards me menacingly. I had dodged the first swipe but he'd landed the next one. I had no choice but to stand my ground, so I grabbed him in a headlock and there he remained while I landed a few punches of my own in the middle of the ring that the other students had formed around us.

A teacher patrolling the yard had eventually

separated us and we were whisked off to the principal's office to be interrogated. I didn't get into any trouble once I had explained my innocence and how the fight developed.

At the end of that school day, I had packed my bag and got ready to walk home. As soon as I had come out the front door of the school, I spotted my sparring partner and all his cronies standing around in a pack. My spider sense had tingled straight away. I had quickly calculated that they would have to let me go around the back of the building, which was my usual route home, because there were teachers out at the front of the school. I had strolled casually along until I got around that first corner. As soon as I was out of sight, I had sprinted as fast as I could. By the time they'd followed, I was a good 300 yards away and on the other side of the boundary fence. I knew they were never going to catch me, so I took a moment to catch my breath and raise my two middle fingers up in the air.

By September 2002, I was had been ready to go into second level at the Donahies Community School. My teacher, Mr Hackett, had tried to convince my mother to send me to Belvedere College, a private school in Dublin city centre, but that was never the way in our family. Mr Hackett was an amazing mentor who had made me eager to learn. Academically he was the most influential character in my life and he really took pride in seeing children develop as individuals.

We were an average working-class family and every man on both sides had left school early to become a skilled worker – builders, plasterers, etc. – but, ever since I was very young, I'd known that was not going to be my calling. I had always been open with my parents, from a young age, about my desire to find a different career path, but I suppose it did make me feel like the odd one out. Going to a private school would have added to that.

Despite turning down my teacher's school recommendation, I will always be grateful for how he nurtured my love of reading. The public library was only a short walk away from our school, and Mr Hackett would take the class over regularly to get whatever books we wanted. One day, he passed me a piece of paper with a number of titles he recommended, and by the end of my final year in primary school, I had read the entire *Lord of the Rings* trilogy, among others. Tolkien's use of language had fascinated me in particular, and if I didn't know what a word meant I looked it up in the dictionary and wrote it down in a notebook. I had been happy in my own little world.

It was at about this time that I had discovered *Harry Potter*, and when the fifth book was published, *Harry Potter and the Order of the Phoenix*, I had my copy pre-ordered in the local shop as I eagerly anticipated its release. When it finally arrived I was absolutely spellbound by it. I read that book from the time I got out of bed in the morning until my eyes closed at night for two days straight until I finished it – much to my mother's dismay. Then I started reading it all over again, if a bit more slowly.

At the time, I was around the same age as Harry in the stories and I really identified with the character that J.K. Rowling had created. It was part of my growing up – I'm sure I am not alone in that – and it was love at first sight when it came to Emma Watson portraying Hermione on the big screen. As well as her amazing looks, I adored the intelligence that her character displayed in the series and the resilience she showed to others when she was mocked for her abilities.

Unfortunately, unlike Hermione successfully settling into the Hogwarts School of Witchcraft and Wizardry, I never felt at home in my new secondary school, and part of that was down to my love of reading, which didn't seem to be shared by many of my new classmates – not publicly anyway. I was friendly with four others from Holy Trinity National School who had joined me at second level, and I got to know new friends through our shared passion for sport. But then one of the lads I went to primary school with began to bully me.

I couldn't understand why in a new school, surrounded by all sorts of new people, he had chosen to target me. I said nothing and hoped it would pass, but it didn't. One day I opened my locker to find a note that read: 'You're a faggot.' He said that I was gay because I often used my free classes to read!

It only got worse when he learned that I was turning down the advances of a girl in our year who had taken a shine to me. It was an attempt to belittle me that went unseen by everyone else, but it upset me deeply. It was a word that passed – and still passes – as an insult, and as disgraceful as that is in today's world, it was too much for a 12-year-old to handle.

I snapped one day when we were walking home after he landed one insult too many. We went at it until a stranger jumped out of his car and separated us on the side of the road. He never gave me any more trouble after that.

When I had entered this block of counselling, I was desperate to dig deeper into my identity and learn more about who I had been growing up and what had led to my having such a confused sense of who I was now. Recalling that memory was really important: as I remembered what it had been like to take a stand for who I really was. But times change, as do people; I was never going to be that same 12-year-old, but at least I knew I had it in me to defend passionately who I was if it came down to it.

There were some high points during that year in school too, like when I got picked to play in a Dublin All-Star game, which saw a carefully selected GAA team from north Dublin schools take on their equivalents from the southside in Parnell Park before the Dublin senior team played Galway in April 2003. It gave me my first sense of what it was like to play in front of big stadium crowds, and I instantly loved the buzz. The sense of pride I got when the crowd cheered after I made a save was extraordinary and unlike anything I had felt before. It was far from the imaginary worlds of my garden goals, or even playing out on the road with friends – and it was addictive. I can see now why a boy would be so desperate to feel that way again.

Although Parnell Park wasn't full that day, for a 12-year-old goalkeeper dreaming of the big time, it was the equivalent of playing in Old Trafford. Little did I know that the next time I'd play there would be eight years later for Cavan in an All-Ireland under-21 semi-final! It was a fine achievement, given that the first time I played a proper GAA game was just a year previously. I remember asking then how many steps you're allowed to take before you have to bounce it or solo it. Despite being a Gaelic football novice, I had learned by then that I had some natural talent in between the posts thanks to soccer.

My grandfather Bill had seen it too when he was explaining one of the basic rules of goalkeeping to me. 'The closer you come to the man with the ball, the smaller the goals gets for him. So the trick is to come out far enough from the line to close him down but not so far that he can lob you,' he explained. We put the theory to the test then, and he fired a couple of balls at me.

'Can you kick them harder, Grandad?' I asked. It was only years later that he admitted to me that he was kicking them as hard as he could!

Goalkeeping fast became my way of life, but few people knew I was also really enjoying something completely different: Irish dancing. At a very early age in primary school it was compulsory for students to take part in the dance class, but that session soon became a bi-weekly passion of mine. At first I got so nervous before performing that I would physically shake, but I stuck with it, and in time I won an All-Ireland medal for my age group at the championships.

Soon, though, my dreams of being a footballer started to clash with dancing, and I was forced to choose between the two because of time constraints. While I decided to leave the dancing shoes in the bottom of the wardrobe for good, I didn't know that I would have to leave everything else in my life behind a few short years later.

After completing my first year in secondary school, my parents dropped the bombshell that we were moving to Cavan. Initially I wasn't at all happy with the idea, but promises of a set of goals in the garden, a trampoline and my own room saw me warm to the idea. Kids are predictable that way. After only weeks of searching, they found the house that would become our home in Cavan. We moved on from Dublin and all that went with it, including school, friends, family and soccer.

While the move was an opportunity for a blank canvas, I had already fixed my bully problem in Dublin and I dreaded starting a new school with the possibility of having to do it all over again. Without realising it, I had sacrificed parts of my true identity, like my love of reading and my engagement in the classroom, in order to fit in to my new environment and avoid standing out from the crowd. My survival instincts took over.

I just wanted to belong to a group, and, over time, my grades became less and less important to me. Soon I was happy to stay between the 60–80 per cent range. I quickly twigged that in Cavan, football could be the key to having a smooth existence, as it would help me slot into my new environment and find the safety of a pack in unfamiliar surroundings. Focusing on it made life easier than reading, studying or dancing ever could.

As the football part of my life went from strength to strength during my first few years in Bailieborough, others began to notice, however, that it was affecting other areas. I never stopped to think about it, as I was happy with friends, and excelling at the sport gave me an easy way to connect with others in school. In 2007, and still just 16, I was juggling my Leaving Cert preparations with getting ready for my first ever Ulster minor championship campaign.

One teacher, Mrs Cunningham, eventually ran out of patience after I had failed to produce my homework yet again, and told me in front of the class that the time had come to decide whether I wanted to be an honours English student or play for Cavan. Usually we had an excellent rapport, but I laughed out loud at her ultimatum.

Little did she know that any night I had training, there wasn't much time for homework after I'd had dinner. A bus would pick up myself and my friend Sean Cooney at 6 p.m. and take us to Kingspan Breffni Park via Virginia, Ballyjamesduff, Mountnugent and Ballinagh. My parents thought the service was fantastic, but it took over an hour to travel to Cavan when it would have taken just 20 minutes by car.

The journey home was the same, so by the time I'd finished training, showered and got fed I wasn't back at my house until 11 p.m. By then, I was fit to collapse into bed, so sometimes the homework got finished and sometimes it didn't. If I could manage it, I would attempt to finish it the next morning over breakfast or, if I could get away with it, while other classes were going on. I did enough to get by and enough to keep my homework problems off my parents' radar.

Those shortcomings never bothered me though, as schoolwork simply couldn't match the buzz I was getting from being part of the Cavan minor panel. But in the meantime I had gone from being an exemplary student in my first year in secondary school to settling for not failing exams by the time my final year came around.

Playing for the county team enabled me to experience something completely new, and, thinking back, I liked the social standing and self-assurance that came with it. My time was further eaten into when I was cast as the intimidating villain Bill Sykes in

Oliver, our school musical. Lines had to be learned and I also had to sing an entire song by myself, but again the social aspect of it was great. The show ran for four nights and was sold out each time. I felt like I'd travelled so far from the fairly solitary individual who sat in class reading books when others were mingling all around; now I was at the centre of it all.

I finished the year with 450 points in my Leaving Cert – a score I was pleasantly surprised with, given that I had failed three of my mock examinations a few months earlier. My mother was shocked when I flunked those maths, biology and accounting mocks and it led to a very direct conversation between us, but I was extremely calm about the whole thing. She was much more worried than I was because I knew I could get through the real thing without much fuss; after all, I'd passed the other four without studying at all. My glass had definitely been half full back then, and I yearned for a drop of that optimism in my current life.

That attitude showed just how much I had changed during my first four years in Cavan as I believe I could have come close to the maximum of 600 points if I really had wanted to. Being in the school musical and getting to play in front of thousands of people in Kingspan Breffni Park brought me more life experience than 100 extra Leaving Cert points ever could, but, at the same time, I still feel I could have found a happier medium. I didn't realise it then, but letting my love of the game get so far ahead of other things on the priority list didn't ultimately work for me. There were other parts of me, the person I was, that needed attention too, and I was now keen to feel as passionately about myself as I had done when standing up to that schoolyard bully.

Playing for the county in the 2007 Ulster minor championship had let me fulfil my dreams of performing in big stadiums and brought me respect that I had never commanded before. My clubmate Cillian Sheridan had already joined Glasgow Celtic at that stage, and word had come back to my mother that one of the scouts was going to check me out during the Cavan campaign, as I was no longer playing soccer due to my Cavan and Leaving Cert commitments. The year before I had been part of a regional squad selected from the underage leagues in Meath, Louth and Cavan that played in the Foyle Cup, one of Europe's top youth competitions. We finished in fifth place, one spot behind the Republic of Ireland squad, and beat a professional club from Holland, before being knocked out on penalties by eventual champions Ferencváros, a professional club from Hungary. Sadly, the Celtic rumours never came to anything and I heard no more about it.

A Leeds United scout had watched me earlier in my youth, only to tell me that I wasn't tall enough, but two years on, in my early teens, I had grown a foot in height and stretched to a size 12 shoe. I thought the Celtic rumours might be a second opportunity to attempt the professional sporting life, and it would have taken a move as huge as that to stall my growing adoration for Gaelic football.

While I had frequently felt like a lost soul in the vast concrete jungle of Dublin, in Cavan I had morphed into a talented, likeable teenager who was valued by his peers. I was a million miles from the innocent child who the bullies had chosen to focus on twice before. My identity had completely changed. To most, I was a happy, confident and talented county footballer, but the only person I was really authentic with and would be open and honest with about feelings and emotions was the girl I had fallen for.

I left school after my Leaving and immediately took up the position in the *Cavan Post*. When I was promoted to sports editor after a number of months my character and make-up again shifted without me realising. It was a lot of pressure and responsibility for a 17-year-old, and I was managing a co-worker more than ten years my senior, so I had to up my professional game to meet the responsibilities of the job. While my friends enjoyed the freedom of student life, I had to learn about managing people, standing firm in my convictions at work, meeting deadlines, editing content and delegating responsibility. I felt I had to put on a front as a leader rather than being a natural at it, and had to justify to my colleagues why I had been given the role at such a young age.

When I went to college in 2008, it made for an odd change. I had tried so hard to be mature, sensible and sophisticated at work, traits which all came naturally to me over time, but I soon learned that that was not what was expected of me when I arrived on the student scene. I tried to be more cavalier and carefree like those around me but I found that transition fairly difficult, and it was something I had to work on.

After being in a position in which I had learned so much and experienced a regular sense of accomplishment, I really struggled to see what more I was going to learn from my journalism course at college. In my last few weeks in the *Cavan Post*, I had felt burned out. I was very much looking forward to the change of lifestyle that college promised but it was a false dawn. I rarely attended lectures, and I considered dropping out many times. When my loving relationship began to hit a rocky patch towards the end of my college stint, and with work no longer an option to distract me, I focused every ounce of my attention on football. As well as playing with my club, college and county, I had become involved with coaching teams in the college and the administration side of things.

The GAA had dominated my life and I reaped so many benefits from it. I met brilliant people through the sport, and achieved social respect and contentment that I never would have imagined as a kid. The scholarships I received along the way helped me to survive financially too. Allowing the sport to absorb my time was the easiest way to hide any emotional hurt and dissatisfaction I was experiencing, particularly following the ending of my relationship – so I superglued the GAA mask to my face until I couldn't do it anymore.

Understanding and fully digesting the heartbreak of the split with my girlfriend helped enormously in being able to drop the mask and be true to myself. I saw how important it was for us to go our separate ways and discover who we were as individuals, away from the comfort that our relationship had brought for so long.

There was no denying that she was an amazing part of my life, and as I reflected on the time we had spent together, I appreciated more than ever what we had. The biggest compliment I can give her is that she made me feel things that I hope to feel again in the future when I fall in love with someone special.

We rarely see each other anymore as our lives have moved down very different paths, but now whenever I think about what we had, I smile because it happened, rather than regret that it's over.

As a man I didn't feel the level of understanding and acceptance that we had together could be replicated by any of my friends back then. For a while, I thought I had to be in a loving relationship to ever feel understood again, but I learned that wasn't true.

The most important thing I realised was that I had to learn to understand myself once more, and for that to happen, a mask could never be placed over my face again.

17
The Fog

My mind had been surrounded by a thick fog for so long, but as I stood on the Golden Gate Bridge in San Francisco, surrounded by actual fog, my mind felt clear for the first time in years.

I leaned against the railing and looked down at the intimidating plunge to the water below. As the waves crashed against the foundations, I thought about all the people who had jumped off in a desperate attempt to escape their inner suffering and emotional pain. I thought about how close I had come to ending my life on two occasions, but the sharp wind that stung my face brought me back to the present moment – just like it had done in my car on the motorway years earlier.

I was on my own, thousands of miles away from home, and I could not recall ever feeling so at peace with myself. On an autumn day on the California coast, my brain was quiet. The absence of internal conversations brought me an incredible amount of satisfaction and pride. After years of questioning the validity of my life, after countless hours discussing thoughts and feelings in counselling sessions and with myself in my head, I had achieved a vital reprieve.

Internal dialogue is part of living; it is something we all have to deal with. Earlier that day, I had gone into a restaurant to get breakfast and spent a number of minutes considering what to order – nobody else in the world knew anything about the conversation that took place, and it was a perfectly ordinary example of how we talk to ourselves on a daily basis. Yet my depression made these chats far more sinister and draining, and at times they felt like temporary spells of insanity.

It was incredibly liberating to realise that I was no longer dependent on football, work or a relationship to feel happy. Of course those things were going to add to my life in the future and bring inevitable ups and downs, but like the men who had built the bridge I was standing on some 80 years earlier, I had the solid foundation that I needed. With that in place, I knew that I could have a long, meaningful and quality life.

Having desperately avoided being alone for so long through playing football, going out drinking, coaching teams and calling over to friends on free evenings, I had travelled halfway around the world with just one suitcase of clothes and my laptop for company. I had left my job in SpunOut.ie shortly after my first anniversary because I'd wanted to spend three months working on this book and experience regular sunshine and a different culture.

I departed with a great sense of fulfilment after significantly growing the audience of SpunOut, an organisation I passionately believe in. When I began my role, social media was acquiring just eight per cent of the hub's monthly readers but by the time I left, more than one third of the total readers who used the service were accessing it through the social media channels I was managing. That increase meant the site was also reaching an average of 100,000 readers per month for the first time, a substantial increase on previous years, so the information the team worked so hard to collect and maintain was reaching more young Irish people than ever before. It was an achievement that brought us a great sense of satisfaction as we all worked there in the hope that we could empower young people to live happier, healthier lives.

The team atmosphere we had in the office was such a welcome change from the GAA dressing rooms I was so accustomed to, where the men, myself included, often used their amazing capacity to say so much without saying anything at all. I let my guard down in this more open, communicative environment, and became extremely comfortable in my own skin over time.

That role, in an incredible organisation, allowed me to assist young people in finding whatever information they needed in their day-to-day lives, but while I was helping others to educate themselves for the better, I still had a lot of learning to do myself.

I had considered travelling on a number of occasions previously, but I was glad that had never come to pass. If I had headed for the departure lounge back then, there is no doubt that I would have been running away from my problems and delaying a process that needed to happen, and needed to happen at home with the support of close friends and family.

The time was right for me in 2015, and rather than clinging to the support networks I had built up to deal with life's inevitable challenges, I was determined to challenge myself even more and continue to grow.

Thankfully I had learned to open up and be transparent with friends like Niall Kelly, Danny Hanley, Niall O'Reilly, Shane Gray, Colm Smith, Barry Tully, Sean Cooney, Shane Donnellan, Declan Lally, John Buckley and others over the years.

For so long, I had fretted about how people would look at me differently once I admitted I suffered with depression, but working against that only strengthened my bond with my closest friends, my parents and my brothers.

My relationship with football has also changed. Simply put, it no longer defines who I am as a person. I found it difficult to watch the Cavan team go about their business in 2015, and there was hardly a day that went by without my thinking about the camp in some form, but I never regretted my decision to walk away.

I seized control of my life again and I started doing what I wanted, when I wanted.

With the time and distance that my trip to America allowed me, I learned to truly value my own company once more – just like when I was a kid.

I never had a set schedule while I was in America, which was completely liberating. I woke up each morning and decided how I wanted to seize the day. I was relaxed and at peace, and it felt incredible. I spent days strolling around different parts of the city with just my headphones and laptop for company. I was living in the moment, and doing it without the structure or support of a team.

Even simple things like eating lunch or dinner on my own in restaurants, or going to the cinema by myself, started to feel normal to me. I lay about soaking up the sunshine, reading books or trying to write this one. I wasn't worrying about what other people thought of me, and that in itself was huge progress.

One statistic that always stuck with me was that one out of four people have depression, and I never thought I would be the one. I learned that a much better way to look at it is that four out of four of us have mental health; sometimes we feel good and other times we don't. It's just part of life, and it can be fed for better or worse by what we tell ourselves, and how other people react to us.

While the depths of depression can be abysmal, becoming more aware of my mental health, even when times are good, will certainly help me avoid more serious incidents down the line. I try to keep up with it as a habit, so every day I rate my mood from one to ten, and I think about the little things that I can do to get me moving towards the upper end of the scale. Things like going to the cinema with a friend instead of sitting at home alone watching a movie can help, as can getting on my bike and going for a cycle along the coast instead of lying in bed. I love taking in the fresh air that blows in from the sea. I get in touch with my friends and go for food or a quiet drink in an environment that enables me to enjoy worthwhile and meaningful conversations.

These simple choices can work for me, but if I struggle for an extended period, I know I can call Niall at any time and step back into that room in search of understanding. Despite my initial resistance to opening up to that process and fearing that I would be placed in a straitjacket, I have learned that counselling works for me, and being able to trust that process is incredibly empowering.

There is no doubt that the GAA is a unique organisation, and it has certainly been a huge part of my life. Playing for my county provides a fantastic opportunity to experience moments and atmospheres that many can only dream about. It is a platform where I can become a hero to peers, a role model to others and feel a bond with those around me that few ever experience in the daily grind. However, to rely solely on that identity is not healthy, because with sport there have to be winners and losers, and as an individual I had to learn to recognise and appreciate the other strands of my life and personality.

I will be forever grateful for the memories associated with pulling on that Breffni jersey and going to battle with some wonderful characters who will remain lifelong friends. I have faced many low points already in my young life, but playing for Cavan has also brought me many unforgettable highs.

The demands placed on players in the modern game are unprecedented, and so many have questioned whether it's all worthwhile. I believe that more and more players will walk away from the game or fall out of love with it unless there is a radical overhaul of the GAA season as we currently know it. The balance is all wrong and because of this, unprecedented demands are also being placed on the services provided by the Gaelic Players Association.

The training-to-games ratio is so heavily biased towards the former it defies both logic and belief and the poorly managed overlapping of club and inter-county seasons means the best players barely get any downtime. In the long term, it is unsustainable and it is something the powers that be in the GAA need to address urgently.

There are personal and professional sacrifices that I chose to make, but the physical demands began to take their toll on my mind and body too. At 24 years of age, I had broken my arm twice in such a way that I can't throw a ball without pain in my wrist. I've had two surgeries in my groin and an operation to install a cable and bolt into my ankle to prevent it from continually collapsing. Three times I've had steroid injections pumped into my body to settle injuries; I've torn a hamstring and quad; and I've experienced enough hip discomfort to wonder how that joint is going to cope later in life.

Yet ironically, while in America, the farthest away from Cavan football I had ever been, I came back to the game in a new way, and learned to appreciate it again for many of the right reasons.

I contacted Brian Reilly, the manager of the Sons of Boru/Celts team before I travelled and asked if they could help to accommodate me for the summer. They were a well-known GAA club in San Francisco and a lot of my friends from the Cavan under-21 team, the likes of Shane Gray and Kevin Meehan, had featured for them in the past. They all spoke positively about their experiences and the warm welcome they received. It also helped that there was a strong Cavan connection with Brian, who has feisty Mullahoran blood pumping through his veins. He went out of his way to find me a place to stay for three months and integrate me into the team for the summer.

When I landed in the States, I was only hoping for a room of my own in a quiet house, but I found a home away from home. Brian paired me up with his good friend and my would-be teammate Andy Fogarty in a gorgeous house just on the edge of downtown

San Francisco. I can't thank Andy and his partner Lisa enough for the hospitality, kindness and warmth they showed me throughout my stay. Andy was born and raised Stateside, but his dad had been an All-Ireland winner with Tipperary before emigrating, so the GAA was engrained in his consciousness. They truly made me feel like one of their own and the only real expense I incurred while staying in their house was from the loss of socks to their amazing dog, Spud.

Training and playing with the team in San Francisco was a wonderful way to meet new people, and I encountered some great men. My short settling-in period was made all the easier by the arrival of Conor McClarey, one of my Cavan colleagues when we won the Ulster under-21 championship in 2011. He had come on as a substitute in Croke Park to score a goal in the All-Ireland final against Galway, and he added plenty more throughout the summer as we secured the San Francisco intermediate championship.

I played six games for the team during that run, chipped in with a few long-range points from frees and conceded no goals. Just like I had always wanted, my inner game reflected my outer game and I was a happy character on and off the field. Regardless of the saves I made and the fact I felt I was performing as well as I had done in years, that was my real achievement.

Playing out there rarely felt like a chore, and I enjoyed it for what it was – a hobby. It helped that the training to games ratio was much better too. It was a return to a bygone era, and I attended every gathering with the Boru/Celts except during the two weeks I spent on the road with Danny Hanley and Niall Kelly, my two close friends from home. Together we travelled to Las Vegas, Los Angeles and San Diego, and it was such an unforgettable time. Throughout those 14 days, with the company of people from home for the first time in months, I was never more myself. I felt calm and assured. I was relaxed and had rediscovered my sense of humour. I was the person I had been searching for.

It was in complete contrast to how I had felt a year earlier when I had withdrawn from the Cavan panel in a state of total personal crisis. I had sunk so low during that spell that I'd needed antidepressants for the first time. Thanks to counselling, I knew a daily tablet was not going to be a miracle cure that made all my problems go away, but it helped to give me enough drive to make survival that little bit easier during an abysmal time.

Since that spell, there have been so many good days in my life, as well as plenty of bad ones. Every now and again the little voice in my head still does everything in its power to entice me to hide from the world, but I usually win. Of course I wish depression had never entered my life and that I could have avoided all the misery that came with it. However, I do not regret my journey. My recovery path has brought with it a sense of enlightenment and perspective that I will be forever grateful for.

I now know that the GAA is and always will be part of who I am, but since 2014 I have worked hard to forge my own identity away from the sport I grew up worshipping. Who knows what the future will hold in that regard.

I need to make it clear that I am not a mental health expert. All I know is what happened to me. The effect of my depression was difficult to get to grips with and I could see no way out from a very dark place. Thankfully I have lived to tell the tale, and I am proud to have shared it over the course of these pages.

This book is a real person telling a real story. It is about encountering depression for the first time and trying to ignore it, fight it and resist it. It is also about how I had to embrace the dark cloud over my head and learn to look for answers from within, rather than seeking a quick fix in the form of football, work, a relationship, alcohol or medication. It's about the highs and lows of life and the endless wonderings of a depressed mind as it tries to decide between continuing the fight or giving up.

For years, I had felt like a prisoner in my own brain, but as I looked out over Alcatraz, the world's most famous penitentiary, I couldn't help but feel hopeful knowing I was once again an authentic version of myself. I wanted to be the best person that I could be, but it dawned on me that the best person I can be is myself.

Knowing that I was returning to Ireland the following week, I casually strolled off the Golden Gate Bridge with a broad smile on my face because I was certain of one thing.

The best is yet to come.

Epilogue

My slide into depression was a gradual one after the All-Ireland final in 2011. In the six months thereafter, I ignored all the signs, mental and physical. I regularly turned a blind eye to any opportunity to reach out for help and to connect with those around me because I didn't know how to describe how I was feeling. I let fear of the stigma of mental health problems overpower me, and kept it all to myself because I didn't want to be seen as weak.

It didn't need to be that way – and that's why I wrote this book.

The darkest point of my depression was the moment my brain sought to take advantage of my uncertainty about everything and urged me to crash my car into the wall. My own mind presented suicide as a logical way for me to end the internal debate that questioned my existence so persistently. I benefitted so much from the conversation with my mother later that same evening, where I openly admitted for the first time that I was suffering with depression, and from there I was pointed towards the professional help I needed.

It only takes one conversation to turn things around. That drive home was me hitting rock bottom, but I wish I hadn't needed to sink so low before reaching out for help. Counselling was the most enlightening and empowering experience of my life. I learned so much about myself and about depression in general. I understood that we all have feelings and emotions, and I learned to accept that sometimes they will be happy, sometimes sad. That is just part of life, and the world we live in throws up many challenges – it is not all sunshine and rainbows. Talking with my mam, letting down my shield and defences, was my first step on the road to recovery. The lessons I have learned since, particularly the self-awareness skills, during the many good and bad days, have transformed my life.

Help comes in different forms. It can be a conversation with someone you trust. It can be picking up the phone to call – or text – the Samaritans or Pieta House. It can be a visit to a trusted website like SpunOut.ie to get supportive information. Any number of things can be the first step towards understanding depression, anxiety and any number of other concerns that we too often try to hide from others for fear of being judged.

It is okay not to feel okay – and absolutely okay

to ask for help. Trust me, I learned the hard way. Remember, should you ever feel like I did, you don't have to tell everyone. Just tell one person; someone you trust. Open up to a parent, a friend, a boyfriend, a girlfriend, a brother, a sister, a teacher or a coach. Depression tries to make you feel like you are the only person in the world to feel that way but it is simply not the case.

I urge anyone who is struggling or in difficulty or feeling suicidal to tell a loved one, contact your GP, visit the nearest A&E or engage with a support service. At the end of this book, I've included contact details for some of the services that are available.

If you are worried about someone you care about, I encourage you to ask the direct questions: Are you feeling depressed? Are you okay? Do you need someone to talk to? Say the words. To ask a person how they are and then to truly listen to them is one of most powerful things you can do in a world that is so consumed by busyness.

If a friend seems distant, go out of your way to catch up with them, even if they knock you back a few times. You don't have to fix all their problems for them, you just have to turn up. If they want to open up to you, they can. Just enable them to feel heard, and point them in the right direction if they do; let them know you are there for them, just like my mam did.

Be open to counselling, and encourage others to be open to it. The best part of my counselling experience was rediscovering myself and allowing the real me to emerge from behind the many masks I had collected. I learned that happiness is an inside job. What's more, rather than making them more difficult, being open and honest about my feelings has strengthened my relationships with the people I care about. Having that support network, and not feeling obliged to lie or hide what I am thinking, is incredibly powerful and liberating.

Since returning to Ireland from the States I've definitely become a more resilient, compassionate and understanding person. My struggle with mental health has been tough work at times; there were so many ups and downs, and it has taken me years to truly find my way. I can only hope that my being honest about all of that within these pages can help someone who is confused, living in a dark place or consumed by depression.

I don't think I have changed much as a person throughout it all, but I have certainly added layers to who I am. And I have without doubt altered the way I deal with disappointments, how I process my thoughts and feelings and how I communicate with my friends and family. I have learned to be a better version of myself and I am really proud of that. It has transformed my life, carried it from a place of despair to one of hope.

On the back of that achievement, I returned to the Cavan panel for the 2016 season and my relationship with the game is infinitely better. It was nice to be welcomed back by the management and my teammates with open arms; in people like Gearoid McKiernan, Niall Murray, Niall McDermott I have made friends for life thanks to football. In a weird way, it felt like I was never away because I integrated back into the group immediately but, just like myself, the team had also evolved and matured. I enjoyed helping my county secure promotion to the top division of the football leagues – exactly where I dreamed of getting all those years ago.

I also formed a good bond with the other goalkeeper, Ray Galligan, over the course of the season and we definitely helped each other, along with the guidance and support from trusted mentor Gary Rogers. Football is a hobby for me now, and being honest, while I still devote a huge amount of time to it and care greatly about the game, I have to say that it is not the most important thing in my life anymore. I like playing football, I like being part of a team because there is strength in numbers, but I'm not sure I will ever love the game the way I once did. I think I am finally okay with that because there is more to my life than football, and I have achieved what I wanted for so long – balance.

Sometimes change is easy, but sometimes it can be really, really hard. So hard, in fact, that we can wonder if things will ever get better. True change requires persistence: it's often one step forward, two steps back, particularly with anything as delicate as our mental health.

People who are struggling with their mental health are not numbers or statistics on spreadsheets. We are real people, and sometimes we lose our way. I only began to find myself again when I realised how lost I was, and how much I needed help. The right services and supports need to be in place to help the many others who will go through similar problems.

In Ireland we have shown again and again that we can create meaningful change. Before I went through all of this, I doubted whether attitudes and perceptions towards mental health would ever change in our country, but through my own experience, I've learned how open-minded people can be.

It's easy to blame our political leaders and decision-makers for the current mental-health crisis in our country, but as a nation that has contributed so much through literature, music, sport, science, business and technology, we must now seize the power we all possess as individuals to demand and create change.

Just look at how attitudes towards smoking in pubs, drink-driving and marriage equality have changed in the past 20 years. Mental health and the wellbeing of our people is the next thing we have to address. Of course we need our leaders to help us, but we cannot sit back and rely on them. We all must work together and, bit by bit, conversation by conversation, we can make Ireland a more compassionate and understanding place. Try starting a conversation with your family and friends about mental health – whether or not you're struggling at the moment yourself.

More and more meaningful conversations are beginning to take place. Schools are leading the way, taking the initiative and ignoring the lack of direction from policy-makers by working with organisations like Cycle Against Suicide to educate our young people on the importance of wellbeing in a fun and engaging way. Students and teachers are not waiting for the change to happen, they *are* the change.

Let there be no doubt that the tide is turning. In 2016 I founded my own organisation called Real Talks, as I passionately believe that learning how to have meaningful conversations with those around us will help us to live happier and healthier lives.

Through workshops and presentations in schools, organisations and communities, I've been sharing my own experiences with depression in order to start a dialogue. Together we discuss our vulnerabilities and communication problems. We listen to each other. We examine together how to build our confidence and resilience in the face of setbacks.

My strongest memory of witnessing real change came during a visit to Abbey Grammar School in Newry. I had spent some time explaining how one of my biggest and most difficult achievements was learning how to embrace vulnerability instead of trying to bury it deep within me.

With a group of lads I discussed the themes running through a chapter of this book, the moment when I finally let go and let the tears flow after being suppressed for far too long. I felt I had their full attention as we talked it through, and I sensed that we were making a strong connection. I stopped for a second to gather my thoughts. I had an urge to ask a question, but I wasn't sure if I should.

I scanned the room and decided to go for it. 'Lads, would anyone in this room admit to having cried in the past year?' I asked.

I knew that there was no way I would have put my hand up for that when I was a student. The room fell silent. The boys sneaked looks at each other to see what the others were doing. I knew I had put them on the spot, but I was curious and I wanted to push the boundaries with them. I saw a young man at the front of the room lift his arm halfway up before he realised nobody else behind him had done it. He quickly put his hand back down.

I was getting ready to move on, about to accept that I had gone a step too far, when the same fella shot his hand up again. He kick-started a chain reaction and, after 15 seconds or so, half of the group had their hands in the air. It blew me away. It was one of the most satisfying moments in my life. I knew I had witnessed real and meaningful change. The lads looked around the room and realised that the walls hadn't caved in because they embraced their own vulnerabilities. In that moment, they had taken a step towards accepting that the ordinary pitfalls of life, such as relationship break-ups, bereavements, exam stresses and losing matches can all weigh us down, but it's perfectly normal because it shows we care.

That moment showed me that while we are not where we need to be just yet, we are on the right path. We are getting there, and if these young people are the future, then we will be in a stronger, more understanding and compassionate place in years to come.

Hundreds of people die by suicide each year in Ireland and thousands more continue to suffer in silence, but I believe the tide is turning. We must all embrace it.

Start a revolution in your family, with your friends, in your school, college or workplace. Change the way we communicate. Be more truthful and honest. Shatter the silence. Be the change. Break down the walls of stigma, one conversation at a time.

The best is yet to come – for all of us.

Resources & Contact Details

Below are the contact details for some – but certainly not all – of the wonderful mental health organisations in Ireland.

Start by talking to your GP, a friend, a family member or an adult you trust.

If you'd like some impartial, friendly and confidential advice for you or someone you care about, get in touch:

Pieta House
www.pieta.ie

Pieta House works to help people who are self-harming or suicidal, and for people who are worried about friends and family who are self-harming or suicidal.

Pieta House has centres around the country, so check the website for the phone number of the centre nearest you.

Pieta House is also on Facebook, Twitter, Instagram and YouTube.

SpunOut.ie
www.spunout.ie

SpunOut.ie provides young people with up-to-date, factual information on wellbeing and maintaining good physical and mental health, free of any shame or bias.

Text (087) 773 0000 and one of the team will reply during office hours.

E-mail info@spunout.ie and they will get back to you within 48 hours – but often much quicker!

Phone (01) 675 3554 during office hours.

SpunOut.ie is also on Facebook, Twitter, Snapchat, Instagram and YouTube.

The Samaritans
www.samaritans.org

The Samaritans are there to listen to you and help you talk through your concerns, worries and troubles. When you call, they will give you an opportunity to talk about any thoughts or feelings you have, whatever they may be.

The Samaritans are there 24 hours a day, 365 days a year. If you need a response immediately, it's best to call on the phone – it's a FREE call.

Phone 116 123 (ROI) or 116 123 (UK)

Email jo@samaritans.org

The Samaritans are also on Facebook, Twitter, YouTube, Google+ and LinkedIn.

~

If you think your school or youth group could benefit from talking about mental health, get in touch:

Cycle Against Suicide
www.cycleagainstsuicide.com

The main objective of the Cycle is to raise awareness of the considerable help and supports that are available for anyone battling depression or self-harm, at risk of suicide or those bereaved by suicide. The 'Ask for Help' section of their website has a great list of organisations to contact for urgent help.

Phone (086) 180 5898
Email info@cycleagainstsuicide.com

Cycle Against Suicide is also on Facebook, Twitter, YouTube and Instagram.

Real Talks
www.realtalks.ie

Real Talks is a dynamic organisation founded by Alan O'Mara to facilitate discussions on the importance of mental health, effective communication, personal leadership and resilience. They specialise in sparking impactful and measurable 'real talks' within the workplace, schools, sports teams and in other communities.

Get in touch via the contact form on the website or email info@realtalks.ie

Acknowledgements

The problem with acknowledgments is where to start, and how to avoid leaving anyone out who has helped me on my journey so far.

So many people, some of whom you will have read about in the book, have played important parts in my life, be they teachers, coaches, friends, family or teammates, but I am grateful to each and every one who has had a positive impact and added value in their own unique way.

Thank you to all in the Gaelic Players Association, and in particular Siobhan Earley, for the unwavering support you have provided since I turned to you in my hour of need. You helped me to see that I am so much more than just a footballer, and to believe in my potential as a person. For that, I will be forever grateful.

Thank you to Niall Muldoon, who was a beacon of hope during my darkest times. You helped me learn so much about myself, depression in general, and to look within for answers rather than blaming external factors. Those lessons will stick with me for the rest of my life.

Thank you to Fran O'Reilly of Amaze, who continues to be an inspiring mentor. Your optimism, kindness, creativity and wisdom are a constant source of comfort as I try to be the best that I can possibly be and soar higher than ever before.

I would like to thank all my managers and teammates so far who believed in me, particularly those who shared my passion for changing the fortunes of Cavan football. We have shared some unforgettable highs together and they will live long in my memory.

A special thank you to my former goalkeeping coach and boss Paul O'Dowd for developing my potential on and off the field. I was lucky to find a Mr Miyagi to my 'Daniel-san' in my formative years.

Deciding to travel to America to write a book was a leap of faith but there is no way the writing process would have been so fruitful without the help of Damian Lawlor, Emma Fay, Tricia Purcell, John Buckley and Arthur Sullivan. Each of you asked questions and helped to provide key insights that makes this book such an accurate reflection of my personality and life experiences. I will always be grateful for your time, knowledge and expertise.

Thank you to Brian Reilly in San Francisco, all involved with the Sons of Boru GAA Club, and especially Andy and Lisa Fogarty for providing an

Alan O'Mara

amazing home away from home when I needed a place to write this book.

Thank you to Ciara Doorley and all involved with Hachette Ireland for seeing the potential in my story and believing in it. Your professionalism and knowledge ensured that this is a book of which I am extremely proud, and hopefully, by working together, we have helped people achieve a greater understanding of mental health and wellbeing.

There are too many friends to mention, but thank you in particular to Danny Hanley, Niall Kelly and the rest of 'the lads' who continue to be loyal and trustworthy friends. You all know who you are!

Finally, and most importantly, I want to thank all my family, and in particular my parents, Carol and Michael, and my brothers, Billy and David, for their unconditional love through good times and bad.